Asian Teachers in British Schools

Multilingual Matters

Citizens of This Country: The Asian British
    MARY STOPES-ROE and RAYMOND COCHRANE
Continuing to Think: The British Asian Girl
    BARRIE WADE and PAMELA SOUTER
Coping with Two Cultures
    PAUL A.S.GHUMAN
Education of Chinese Children in Britain and the USA
    LORNITA YUEN-FAN WONG
Equality Matters
    H. CLAIRE, J. MAYBIN and J. SWANN (eds)
Foundations of Bilingual Education and Bilingualism
    COLIN BAKER
Immigrant Languages in Europe
    GUUS EXTRA and LUDO VERHOEVEN (eds)
Language Diversity Surveys as Agents of Change
    JOE NICHOLAS
Language, Minority Education and Gender
    DAVID CORSON
Making Multicultural Education Work
    STEPHEN MAY
Opportunity and Constraints of Community Language Teaching
    SJAAK KROON
The Step-Tongue: Children's English in Singapore
    ANTHEA FRASER GUPTA
Three Generations, Two Languages, One Family
    LI WEI

Please contact us for the latest book information:
Multilingual Matters Ltd,
Frankfurt Lodge, Clevedon Hall, Victoria Road,
Clevedon, Avon BS21 7SJ, England.

MULTILINGUAL MATTERS 105
Series Editor: Derrick Sharp

Asian Teachers in British Schools

A Study of Two Generations

Paul A. Singh Ghuman

MULTILINGUAL MATTERS LTD
Clevedon • Philadelphia • Adelaide

With Love to Therésa, Shauna and Nalini

Library of Congress Cataloging in Publication Data

Ghuman, Paul A. Singh (Paul Avtar Singh), 1936-
Asian Teachers in British Schools: A Study of Two Generations/Paul A. Singh
Ghuman (Multilingual Matters: 105).
Includes bibliographical references and index.
1. Minority teachers–Great Britain–Case studies. 2. Asians–Great Britain–Case
studies. 3. Discrimination in education–Great Britain–Case studies.
I. Title. II. Series: Multilingual Matters (Series): 105.
LC3736.G6G48   1995
371.1′008693–dc20   94-29845

British Library Cataloguing in Publication Data

A CIP catalogue record for this book is available from the British Library.

ISBN 1-85359-261-7 (hbk)
ISBN 1-85359-260-9 (pbk)

Multilingual Matters Ltd

UK: Frankfurt Lodge, Clevedon Hall, Victoria Road, Clevedon, Avon BS21 7SJ.
USA: 1900 Frost Road, Suite 101, Bristol, PA 19007, USA.
Australia: P.O. Box 6025, 83 Gilles Street, Adelaide, SA 5000, Australia.

Printed and bound in Great Britain by the Longdunn Press, Bristol.

Contents

Foreword

This book is about Asian teachers. It describes their professional hopes, fears, sentiments, aspirations and frustrations at working in British schools. The narrative of this monograph is different to that of many books on education in that the method used for collecting data here is essentially qualitative. A lot of space has been given to the remarks, comments and analysis of the teachers who took part in the study. In a way there are several authors of this monograph — all the teachers and head teachers who were interviewed for this research.

The Commission for Racial Equality (Ranger, 1988) published a research report on the position of ethnic minority teachers. The researcher found that the ethnic minority teachers, as compared to the whites, were less likely to be promoted and were concentrated in the teaching of the shortage subjects of maths, science, and special needs. They generally felt that their career development had been affected by racism in schools and by racial prejudice from their white colleagues. It is a large scale study with an emphasis on quantitative reporting of the data, though there were some comments of teachers on various aspects of their professional roles. Whilst the findings of the inquiry were useful as first stage 'spade-work', more fine-grain analysis of ethnic minority teachers' perceptions and their backgrounds is imperative in understanding the dynamics of inter-cultural encounters in schools.

From my personal experience, it appears to me that the first-generation Asian teachers think that they have not fully realised their professional potential, particularly in securing positions of authority, mainly due to racism in schools. They feel that they have worked hard with the children, acquired the necessary academic and professional skills and contributed generously to the cause of multicultural education. Despite all this, they have not been successful in obtaining posts which are cognate with their qualifications and experience. Ranger (1988: 56–57) illustrated their frustration by relevant extracts from the interview data:

> I have never seen a coloured person in a position of responsibility in my four schools. (white teacher)

Ethnic minority teachers are only given jobs when they cannot find no better teachers — all promotions go to others while we do all the donkey work and are nowhere today. (Indian origin teacher)

On the other hand, most white teachers and some ethnic minority teachers think that there is an equality of opportunity for all. Ranger (1988: 517) quotes a white teacher: 'I find that Asian teachers with whom I have worked often think they are discriminated against because they don't get rapid promotion, when in fact it's due to lack of ability'.

In view of these conflicting perceptions I planned this investigation to illuminate these areas of professional concern. The study is confined to Asian teachers mainly because of the constraints of resources and time. Also I wanted to get to grips with the inner feelings and thoughts of my respondents and felt it might help if I were to choose teachers of my own ethnic group with whom I will have shared similar experiences. I am well aware of the limitations of this stance e.g. subjectivity, projection and self-interest, but as the main plank of the research is ethnographic, personal knowledge of and long standing involvement with, Asian teachers were considered to be advantageous .

I am one of those teachers who migrated to Britain in 1959 and after a spell of bus conducting in Maidenhead got a teaching job in Birmingham. I taught for seven years in secondary modern and grammar schools and read for a Master's degree in education before becoming a lecturer in education. I now teach multicultural education and educational psychology in a university department of education. I am in full agreement with the sentiments of Isaiah Berlin who wrote (1990: 38):

To judge one culture by the standards of another argues a failure of imagination and understanding. Every culture has its own attributes, which must be grasped in and for themselves. In order to understand a culture, one must employ the same faculties of sympathetic insights with which we understand one another, without which there is neither love nor friendship, nor true human relationships.

A group of 25 Asian teachers (referred to as 'first-generation'), who mostly migrated to the UK in the sixties and seventies, were interviewed in-depth (mainly non-directive) to find out their motives for migration, their problems of obtaining teaching jobs in Britain, their subsequent experience of teaching, difficulties they encountered in career advancement, attitudes to their white colleagues and their analysis and comments on a range of multicultural matters.

Another group of 25 Asian teachers who had their qualifications from the British universities and polytechnics (referred to as 'second-generation') were also interviewed to compare their perceptions with that of the first-generation. These groups were not chosen randomly, and they are not a representative sample of the Asian teachers in British schools. The majority were contacted through an Asian teachers' Association in the Midlands and the rest were known to me during my 30 years of professional work in schools and teacher training establishments. To give a broader base to the data a number of white classroom and senior teachers and a few Afro-Caribbean teachers were also included in the inquiry. The interview data is supplemented with my personal impressions and informal discussions with teachers, head teachers, multicultural advisors, colleagues in the department of education and Asian parents and pupils. In my view, the approach adopted here is very close to an ethnographic perspective in which emphasis is placed on the qualitative aspects of the data. Ethnography is particularly associated with ideas such as *the importance of understanding the perspectives of the people being studied* and of observing ordinary everyday activities (Hammersely & Aitkinson, 1983). Some ethnographers even think that it is a form of story-telling (see Walker, 1981).

I have liberally used extracts from the interviews. All interviews, save two, were tape-recorded. I have tried to quote them verbatim, except where I thought the reader might find it difficult to understand comments in this form. In such cases, I have changed the responses minimally to enhance readability and comprehension. Likewise with those interviewees who preferred to switch codes from, say, English to Punjabi/Urdu/Hindi, I have used my discretion to make small changes. I should say at this point that the selection of comments for quotations is essentially a subjective exercise, but an attempt was made to give voice to differing opinions and perspectives. The over-riding aim was to be as comprehensive as possible in coverage.

Recent reports of the Commission for Race Relations (Ranger, 1988; CRE, 1989: 2) have expressed concern over the low number of ethnic minority students entering departments of education and colleges of higher education. The CRE gives statistics to support its claim and concludes:

> Not only does this indicate possible racial discrimination but, if it is correct, means that the overall number of ethnic minority applicants is even lower than so far revealed.

In view of the importance of this topic, I thought it would be very useful to include this topic in the investigation.

In Chapter 1, the aims and objectives of the research are stated clearly as are the sample selection, methodology and recording of the data. The chapter contains full discussion on the academic qualifications and school experiences of the first-generation Asian teachers. Details are also given regarding the number of Asian teachers who obtained qualified teacher's status from the DES.

In Chapter 2, problems relating to the recognition of teachers' qualifications are discussed in detail. Comments from Asian teachers representing two different generations are given extensively to compare their experiences of obtaining their first teaching post.

Chapter 3 is a comprehensive one as it gives teachers' views on a rage of multicultural issues. It also includes the perceptions of white and Afro-Caribbean teachers. I have attempted to compare the views of first-generation Asians with those from the second.

Chapter 4 is about the promotion and professional development of Asian teachers. A wide variety of opinions and attitudes was expressed by the interviewees and this is given full expression. I have discussed Asian teachers' concerns in the context of the available research literature, which I found to be very paltry.

The fifth chapter explores the views of respondents on the possible reasons for the poor intake of second-generation Asian young people into teacher training institutions. The comments of teachers in the study throw light on salient factors involved in this situation. Racism in schools emerges as one of the factors which deters young people from entering teaching. This and other emerging factors are discussed and put into the context of known research in this field.

The last chapter presents an overview of the situation of Asian teachers in Britain. In the light of the differing perceptions of Asian and white teachers and the findings of previous research on promotion and related issues, I have tried to put forward some constructive suggestions.

There is a paucity of literature in this important field. I hope my attempt has gone some way towards addressing this situation. It is also my fervent hope that the debate on the recruitment, training and promotion of Asian and other ethnic minority teachers will be conducted within broader parameters of known factors, rather than within a narrow framework of linear causality.

Acknowledgements

I wish to place on record my sincere thanks to all the teachers and head teachers who so willingly gave their time for this research. Without their generous all-round help this project would have been impossible. I am very grateful to all my colleagues at Aberstywyth, the University of Wales, who have helped me with this research: particularly Daniel Chandler, Bob Jones and Rick Lloyd. I am very appreciative of the financial help which I have received from the Faculty of Education, University of Wales, and from the Vice Principal's Research Fund.

1 Introduction

Background to Migration

The post-Second World War immigration into the UK has mainly consisted of people from the Indian sub-continent and from the West Indies (Caribbean), in addition to an ongoing source from Northern Ireland and some refugees from the eastern European countries (Holmes, 1988). The Commonwealth citizens had the right of entry to the British Isles until 1962 when the first immigration law was passed to restrict entry only to those holding vouchers (work permits) from the Department of Employment. These work permits were issued mainly to those applicants who were deemed useful to the employment market in the UK. In this category came doctors, nurses, scientists, engineers and teachers. Also included were cooks, a few priests of Indian and Pakistani religions and people with vocational qualifications.

For instance, a total of 1,113 vouchers were issued to people with special skills in the period 1965–67 (Rose and associates, 1969: 87). Three types of employment vouchers were introduced by the 1962 Act: A for those with specific jobs to come to; B for those who possessed special skills; and C for unskilled workers. The C-type voucher was discontinued in August, 1965.

Primary immigration to the United Kingdom virtually ceased with the passing of the 1971 Immigration Act, which came into force in 1973. This act restricted the entry of dependants and allowed new entrants to take up specific jobs for a limited period of time only. For instance, the management committee of a Gurudwara could apply for a Bhai (priest) position on the grounds that trained priests are not available in England (Fryer, 1992).

Most teachers from the Indian sub-continent emigrated to the UK for economic and financial reasons. A maths teacher (male, first-generation) recounts:

> I was in the Government Service earning 400 rupees — which was all right, but not enough to support a family or to save for the future needs. Also I had met uneducated people returning from England loaded with money and saying how wonderful it was in the UK. I also had a

1

romantic notion of England — the land of Shakespeare, Hardy and Bacon. I applied for a voucher and got it straightaway. I said to my parents I would be back in five years for good with higher qualifications and money in my pocket.

Other teachers related similar stories. A primary teacher (female, first-generation) gave the following account:

I was a lecturer in government college earning a good salary. I was quite happy in my job. Then a friend told me they are giving vouchers to teachers and lecturers, because they are short of teachers in England — there was an advertisement in the papers that England needs 4,800 teachers. At that time I was single and ambitious. I thought that I can go for few years, gain further qualifications, travel and save some money and come back with all my experience and get a very good job. But all my dreams were shattered in England.

A bus driver, former teacher in India, told me his story:

I was a teacher of Punjabi and history in my village school. My salary was very small. I had five children to look after. As you know everything in India is to be paid for...school fees, then college expenses and of course expenses on dowries for girls (he had three daughters). Our headmaster went to England and couldn't settle down there. He did not get a teaching job, and had to work as an unskilled labourer in a foundry. He told me problems of living in the UK...But he said: 'There is a dignity of labour in that country. Workers can earn as much, if not more, than teachers. There is free national health service and schools and colleges do not charge fees'. I thought to myself: well, I may not get a teaching job there, but I can provide for my family a lot better if I leave this low-paid job.

A TESL teacher (male, first-generation) had romantic notions of travel and learning:

A lot of reasons for coming. In the 50s I applied to go to America. I thought I would study and support myself by washing dishes. A friend of mine was in England. He said to me: 'Come to England. You will learn a lot'. My friend went back after a short stay; he didn't like it here...I came to see the world and study.

I personally know very many teachers who took a calculated risk to emigrate to Britain knowing full well that they would not obtain professional work because of their poor English or the fact that they had passed their degree examinations in the medium of Hindi/Urdu.

Teachers are poorly paid in India and Pakistan and have a very low status as compared to the other professions. Some thousands of teachers emigrated to Britain to improve their financial situation and thereby hoped to add to their personal standing and social status in the eyes of their peers and local community.

A former lecturer, Jeane Brand, who taught teachers from the Indian sub-continent in Nottingham University wrote: 'The exact number of Asian teachers then residing in Britain who would be eligible for recognition was not known. But one estimate suggested that the number might be as high as 6,000. Of those who had been granted recognition only a very few were employed as teachers and a substantial number were known to be in employment which was in no way commensurate with their qualifications, previous experience and training' (Brand, 1972: 145).

According to Rose *et al.* (1969: 87), during the two years period 1965–67, a total of 3,519 vouchers were issued to teachers from India and Pakistan. A total of 42,440 vouchers were given, mainly to professional people from India and Pakistan, between 1962 and 1967. There is no breakdown of figures relating to teachers as such, but a rough estimate is that around 8,000 vouchers probably went to teachers during this period alone. The primary immigration from the Indian sub-continent practically ceased in 1973 as the provisions of the 1971 Immigration Act came into force in 1973.

There are no precise figures on the number of teachers who entered Britain before 1973, but my own guess is that the great majority did not register with the DES to have their qualifications approved. As I was informed by a foundry worker, a former teacher in Pakistan:

> I used to teach history and geography in a high school through Urdu, though I was taught in English and I also wrote my exams in English... But my friends told me that there is no chance of getting a post, even though I can be recognised as a qualified teacher. There were always vacancies for science and maths teachers. So I didn't bother. I do heavy work in the foundry, but I earn a good wage. I think I have done all right.

A detailed picture of Indian and Pakistani teachers who were granted qualified status is given by Jackson (1975: 8–9), and the statistics are presented in Table 1.

Table 1 Indian and Pakistani teachers given qualified status from 1962–72

1962	1963	1964	1965	1966	1967	1968	1969	1970	1971	1972
620	630	1628	1725	800	980	418	477	330	300	250

Aims and Objectives

In 1987 a large scale study was carried out by Ranger (1988) for the Commission for Racial Equality. Its findings are mainly reported in a quantitative style, though a selected number of ethnic minority and white teachers was interviewed to probe into the various aspects of teachers' concerns. A literature search on the Asian teachers revealed only a small number of studies to-date (Rakhit, 1989; Singh *et al.*, 1989; Brar, 1991). I thought it was important to study the aspirations, hopes, concerns and anxieties of first-generation Asian teachers who will soon be approaching retirement age. The chief aim of the present research is to understand and explain the dynamics of intercultural encounters in the teaching profession. I also consider it is important to understand the emerging issues within the context of the existing empirical research and literature.

The objectives of the research are different to the study by Ranger (1988) in that the thrust of the enquiry is to explore the attitudes, opinions and perceptions of Asian teachers over a range of professional and personal matters. These may be stated as:

(1) to discover the main reasons for the migration of teachers from the Indian sub-continent;
(2) to find out the main difficulties they faced in seeking employment as teachers;
(3) to record their professional experience of British schooling;
(4) to study the professional experience of second-generation Asian teachers who had their qualifications from UK higher education institutions and universities;
(5) to compare the attitudes and opinions of first-generation and second generation Asian teachers;
(6) to discover the contribution which the teachers might be making in promoting multicultural education and inter-ethnic understanding;
(7) to investigate reasons for the poor recruitment of Asian young people to teacher training institutions.

Sample Selection

The method used for the collection of data was face-to-face in-depth interviews. This technique is very time-consuming and requires a lot of planning and intensive work in transcribing interview material. Therefore it was not possible to have a large number of interviewees as is possible in quantitative studies. The details of the sample are given in Table 2.

Additionally, four first-generation Asian university lecturers, three of

Table 2 Details of the sample

| | First-generation | | Second-generation | | |
	Male	Female	Male	Female	
Asians	18	7	13	12	
Whites	3	3	2	2	
Afro-Caribbean	1	1	1	1	
Total	22	11	16	15	= 64

whom are working in departments of education, were included in the study to widen the scope of research. Also one white university lecturer was interviewed for the study. There are a number of points to be made about the sample. Firstly, the teachers chosen for the study were working in the English Midlands and they voluntarily participated in the research. The researcher's contact with the schools over the last twenty-three years helped matters considerably. Secondly, it is not claimed that the group selected for study is a random or a representative one, but an attempt was made to include teachers of both primary and secondary sectors, and the group had a fair proportion of women teachers in it. Thirdly, the term 'first-generation' refers to those Asian teachers who had their teaching qualifications in their country of origin, though a significant number also went to British universities and colleges to improve their academic standing or to do in-service work. 'Second-generation' refers to those Asian teachers who had either their full schooling or most of their schooling in the UK, and also went to the British polytechnics or universities to gain academic and professional qualifications. In the case of whites, however, 'first-generation' refers to the teachers who are over 45 and in senior management positions and 'second-generation' to teachers who are below 30 and are classroom teachers. Further details of the Asian sample are presented in Tables 3–7.

Of the white sample in the study, two are head teachers, two deputy heads and two senior teachers and four young classroom teachers. The senior white teachers had considerable experience of working with Asian and black teachers. The number of Afro-Caribbean teachers is very small as it is only meant for comparison. The reader's attention is drawn to two further important features of the first-generation Asian sample: 21/25 are over 40; and 20/25 hold 'B' allowance.

Table 3 Details of Asian sample: School type and average teaching experience, in years

	Primary	Secondary	No. of years
First-generation	9	16	21.7
Second-generation	7	18	8.0

Table 4 Details of Asian sample: Age range

	20–24	25–29	30–34	35–40	41–45	46–50	50 +
First-generation	–	–	–	4	6	6	9
Second-generation	7	10	5	3	–	–	–

Table 5 Details of second-generation Asian sample: Teaching subjects

Sciences	Maths	Modern languages	TESL	English	Others
11	2	2	–	–	3

Table 6 Details of first-generation Asian sample: Teaching subjects

Science	Maths	Community language	TESL	Special needs	Others
2	5	4	2	1	2

Table 7 Details of Asian sample: Status in profession [1]

	Heads	Deputy Heads	Senior Teachers	C	B	A	Standard scale
First-generation	2	0	0	2	20	1	0
Second-generation	1	0	1	2	7	3	11

1. A, B, C, D and E were the incentive allowances (A being the lowest and E the highest) in addition to the pay on the standard scale. This pay structure was replaced by a new pay structure in August 1993.

Methodology of Data Collection

Jung (1988: 11) discussed some of the problems of data collection in psychological research in his writings on the 'Archetypes'. He argued: 'Today we are convinced that in all fields of knowledge psychological premises exist which exert a decisive influence upon the choice of material, the method of investigation, the nature of the conclusions, and the formulation of hypotheses and theories. We have even come to believe that Kant's personality was a decisive conditioning factor of his *Critique of Pure Reason*'. I think a Jungian stance is now widely accepted in the social sciences. The present research is no exception to this dictum.

The data for this research were collected through semi-structured interviews. In a semi-structured interview situation, although there are a set of questions to be asked and probed into, the order and sequence are left largely to the interviewee. Furthermore, digressions from the main theme are accommodated, and sometimes encouraged, to gain fresh insight into the issues under discussion. Kerlinger (1970: 469) sums it up succinctly: 'The unstandardised, non-structured interview technique is an open situation in contrast to the standardised, structured interview, which is a closed situation. This does not mean that an unstandardised interview is casual.'

There are a number of advantages in using this interview technique over the more structured questionnaire and attitude scale. Firstly, on sensitive topics, the interviewer can judge the behaviour of the subjects and monitor the questioning accordingly. Secondly, in-depth probing can produce rich illuminative information which is not normally possible in a conventional questionnaire. Thirdly, the interviewer can judge fairly accurately whether the respondents are being honest and are giving reliable information. Finally, in a relaxed situation, the interviewee can reveal new perspectives on the topics under discussion, which have not been considered by the researcher. There were several examples of this happening in my interview sessions. Many investigators have used the interview method with teachers to study their careers and other aspects of their professional concerns (see, Hilsum & Start, 1974; Woods, 1985; Sikes *et al.*, 1985; Maclean, 1992). I have successfully used this method with ethnic minority parents and young students (see Ghuman, 1993, 1991, 1980).

The major weakness of the interview technique is that it is very time-consuming. Therefore only a small representative number can be included in the research. There is also a problem relating to the reliability and validity of the data, though this shortcoming is equally applicable to questionnaires and attitude scales. To enhance the reliability of the data it was considered imperative to gain the full confidence of the interviewees. In the first pace, the aims and objectives of the investigation were made quite clear and the respondents' minds set at rest concerning my motives and intentions in doing this piece of research. Secondly, complete confidentiality was assured to all the interviewees and the fact that I know several teachers in the group personally helped matters. Thirdly, the interviews were conducted in a relaxed and easy manner in order to win the trust of the teachers in the study. Furthermore, if the interviewee did not wish to respond to any particular question(s), no pressure — subtle or otherwise — was put on them to respond. A related point concerns the use of a cassette recorder during the interview sessions. Two teachers (2/64) were not happy with this arrangement. In these cases detailed notes were taken and other impressions added on after the interviews. The interviewees were given the option of answering questions in any of the main languages of the Indian sub-continent. Several (8/25) first-generation teachers spoke bilingually and enjoyed their conversations as they could switch codes according to the topic under discussion. All the teachers in the study were questioned on multicultural matters, promotion prospects, racism, reasons for poor recruitment of ethnic teachers, achievement of Asian pupils, special difficulties of Asian girls, home-school links and Asian parents' involvement, and relations with white/Asian colleagues. In addition, the first-generation Asian teachers were asked about their motivation for emigrating and their experiences of social adjustment and of obtaining first teaching posts in Britain.

Experience of Teaching in India and Pakistan

The first-generation teachers were asked to reflect on their own education and their teaching experience. Most of them were happy to talk candidly about these matters. A maths and science teacher (male, first-generation) described it as follows:

As you know the class sizes are very large — around 50 or so. But I have taught classes of big size in this country, too. But facilities and resources are very poor. There is very little to demonstrate on topics in science and maths. A lot of learning is rote learning — without much understanding. I used to encourage students to commit to memory theorems of geometry and algebraic formulae. This is the way we were taught. The other complicating factor was that in high schools and colleges the medium of instruction was English. Students were struggling to learn English and to expect them to express themselves in English was asking too much. My own higher education was through the medium of English. It was an uphill task. I memorised most of the stuff in mathematics and English novels and a play of Shakespeare — *The Merchant of Venice*.

A TEFL teacher (male, first-generation), formerly a lecturer of English in India, told me an interesting story:

> When I joined the college to teach English, my head of the department advised me to use standard guide books — Sharda, I recall. He said: 'It would be easy for students to follow and they can memorise the set question'. I refused to take his advice and devised my own notes and tried to teach by involving my students actively in my lessons. This was very disturbing to the older hands. I was told that my results would be very poor, because of my teaching. When the results came out my students really did very well. They were astonished...I can still recall the yellowing notes of my older colleagues!

I interviewed a number of Asian parents for another research project to ascertain their views on educational matters (Ghuman, 1993: 102). It is worth quoting their impressions of Indian schooling. A Sikh parent (Trade Union official, age 46) expressed his views strongly:

> Teachers in India are viewed as scary things; even our parents used to say if you don't listen to us, I am going to talk to your teacher and that used to scare the pants off us. They beat us up; we were demoralised. Teacher sitting as a dictator on a chair and us on the ground. Every thing was drilled into us.

A Muslim (white-collar worker, age 42) had a similar experience:

> I have to grow out of the hard discipline; it didn't teach us anything. I came from Gujrat — Pakistan. Teacher would say: 'bring your homework'. If not, you were caned regularly. We were caned a lot. A lot of kids actually dropped out because of this.

A primary school teacher (male, first-generation) had an interesting perspective:

> In Punjab, children respect their teachers, but this is not the case here. There is more discipline and children are pushed...sometimes through fear. Arithmetic is taught as a bitter pill. Standards are definitely higher in mental arithmetic.

An opinion of a young Indian girl is worth quoting at length because she had experience of schooling in India and Britain:

> I would choose a school like this, rather than the one I went to in India. (*Why?*) Freedom: You can talk to teachers and it is a good thing if you want to make progress in your studies...I be missing this school, but

not this country! Here you are free to make choices…Teachers listen to you…less punishment and we don't get any homework, only in some subjects. In India, teachers have the right to hit you, not here. And a lot of homework (in India) and discipline is much better in India.

It became very clear from the interview data that the education which the first-generation Asian teachers had had was very much along the traditional line, where the authority of teachers was very much respected and feared. Discipline tended to be strict and usually secured through harsh methods. The curriculum in primary schools was and still is confined to the 3R's. A great deal of emphasis was/is placed on rote learning. The success or failure of higher education and schools is measured solely by examination results. Mukherjee (1969: 298–299) sums it up: 'All instruction is subordinated to examinations, extinguishing all initiative in the students. Indian examinations, it has been said, are "capricious, invalid, unreliable and inadequate" and "tend to corrupt the moral standards of university life". The student's sole aim has been to pass the examination and to get the stamp of success from the universities. Indeed, Indian markets and book shops are flooded with "notebooks" and "question and answer books".'

And of the teaching methods, he writes: 'Lecturing too frequently takes the form of reading, at dictation speed, from a textbook, or the giving out of set answers to set questions…it has subjected teaching to examinations, thus making it virtually impossible to provide true education and to develop genuine interest in expanding educational horizons and has created temptations to cheating, corruption and favouritism.'

Mukherjee's assessment sounds unduly harsh, but he is making some significant points about the Indian system (this equally applies to the Pakistani system) which will have relevance and implications for the difficulties which are faced by the first-generation Asian teachers in British schools.

Taylor (1990) described the attempt at curriculum reform in Indian schools as follows: 'Change in teaching methods can come about only if the average class size is drastically reduced. Teachers are trained in the theory and practice of almost every conceivable teaching method…but, with over 50 to teach, the younger teacher inevitably succumbs to the advice of older colleagues and settles into a pattern of delivering sermons and a stylised catechism of question-and-answer-exchanges…For the majority of teachers and pupils the textbook and parrot-learning remain the norm, by which many teachers require blind obedience and virtual silence from the children.'

However, he goes on to say that there is an enormous difference between rural and urban schools and public and state schools in their teaching methods and the resources available. As Diane Spencer, correspondent of the Times Educational Supplement (1989), also reminds us: 'In countless other elementary schools children were sitting in rows reciting tables or copying from a blackboard — if they were lucky enough to have them. But this school was different'.

Taylor (1990: 331) also cautions us: 'Few rural schools have adequate or modern furniture and most have only a small blackboard with which to supplement the textbook. Children's work is seldom displayed. However, it is dangerous to over-generalise'.

There has been no investigation known to the researcher which has been carried out to study the attitudes and opinions of Indian teachers on the learning and teaching processes of young children. I carried out a piece of empirical research in 1974 to throw some light on these issues (Ghuman, 1975). The research is described in some detail as the findings are deemed relevant to the theme of this chapter.

The research was planned to study the attitudes of Punjabi trainee teachers to the learning and thinking abilities of children, and to compare their attitudes with those of a comparable sample of British trainee teachers. Two hypotheses were set up: the Punjabi trainee teachers, as compared with the British, are more authoritarian in their attitudes to children; and the Punjabi trainee teachers' perception of the learning and thinking processes of children is significantly different from that of their British counterparts. The Punjabi sample was taken from a well-established university college in a big city.

Forty-nine women and forty-six men completed part of the Minnesota Teachers' Attitude Inventory. In Britain a comparable sample of graduates (40 men and 47 women) completed the same questionnaire. The attitude scale covered the following areas: modern versus traditional outlook on class control; and favourable versus unfavourable attitudes to pupils. The Punjabi women students were found to be more modern as compared to the men. They scored higher on the item: 'children will think for themselves if permitted'; and lower on the items: 'most pupils lack productive imagination, children are usually too inquisitive, and the teacher is usually to blame when pupils fail to follow instructions'. There was no difference between British men and women, except on one item.

Highly significant differences were found between the Indian and the British sample on all, except four items. As the samples differed on 42/46 items, the hierarchy of items which discriminated between the two groups was worked out using the Contingency Coefficient for each item. Five items which came at the top of the hierarchy are given below: 'Some children ask too many questions; children are not mature enough to make their own decisions; a teacher seldom finds children really enjoyable; children must be told exactly what to do and how to do it; a child should be encouraged to keep his likes and dislikes to himself'.

On these items, the British sample expressed strong disagreement, whereas the Punjabi sample was on the agree and strongly agree side of the continuum. There are a few other interesting items on which the two samples differed significantly: the first lesson a child needs to learn is to obey the teacher without question; increased freedom in the classroom creates confusion; children are unable to reason adequately; and it is not practical to base school work upon children's interest.

The differential response pattern of the two groups lends strong weight to the argument that the Punjabi trainee teachers, as compared with the British sample, believe in strict discipline, under-estimate children's abilities and prefer to adopt teaching methods which are based on the pupils' passivity. They do not wish to be involved in the affective life of the children, but expect a high degree of respect and obedience from the students. They are sceptical of children's abilities to think for themselves and to engage in purposeful activities.

Though this research was conducted with trainee teachers and not with practising teachers, it was not unreasonable to extrapolate that the Indian teachers were similar to the student teachers in their outlook and professional attitudes. They were likely to be even more authoritarian and far less child-centred (see Morrison & McIntyre, 1969). Bennet (1976) established a link between teaching styles and scholastic achievement, and has also shown that teaching styles are closely related to the opinions which teachers hold on classroom organisation and the nature of the learning and thinking processes of children. Though the investigation did not probe into the teaching strategies of the future teachers *per se*, it did assess their attitudes to children's learning and classroom organisation. Therefore, it was concluded that their opinions on the scale did provide at least some indication of the ways in which they wished to teach and to build up their relationship with the pupils. In another research with Punjabi children (Ghuman, 1975), I found the children to be docile and willing to learn everything by rote. They rarely, if ever, actively participated in the lessons. This, then, appears to tie in with the expressed authoritarian attitudes of the Punjabi teachers. Of course, teachers are not entirely to be held responsible for this situation as a number of other factors, such as availability of resources and class size, are also implicated in this state of affairs. Furthermore, I made the following observation (Ghuman, 1975: 120): 'This excessive reliance on memory may be due to the fact that children do their class work on slates and *'phatees'* (a rectangular wooden strip with a coating of clay for practising spelling and writing dictation) and therefore have no access to their previous work as they have to continually erase their sums and writings. Thus children are denied both the opportunity to learn from their own work and to revise rules of arithmetic computation etc., and consequently resort to learning everything by rote.'

These views and outlook on learning and teaching are very much part of the experiences of the majority of first-generation Asian teachers who immigrated to Britain in the 60s and 70s. Very often such deeply-held views and attitude orientations caused some problems in their professional work. I will return to these issues later.

2 Recognition of Qualifications and First Appointment

First-Generation

In the first chapter, I discussed some of the salient reasons why a large number of Asian teachers emigrated to Britain. Their educational background was discussed in some detail in order to shed light on their professional concerns and anxieties in this country. Prior to emigration, most of them had very vague ideas about the teaching opportunities in the UK. The vast majority, initially at any rate, ended up doing manual or semi-skilled jobs, the most popular one being the job of a bus conductor.

A university lecturer (male), formerly a teacher, narrated his experience:

> I left India to improve my professional qualifications. (*What in?*) I wanted to be an engineer or a chartered accountant. To start with I was suffering from a culture shock that I couldn't think straight. The main problem was communication...nobody could understand my English. (*What about the weather?*) Oh, that was all right. It was 1959, so to speak an Indian summer that year? It was really demoralising, though I was forewarned about this on the boat I was travelling. This chap asked me what I was thinking of doing in England. I said I would try teaching. On hearing this he roared with a loud laughter, being a city person he spoke with a good accent, and thought I was mad to entertain such an idea with my appalling pronunciation and lack of fluency. The people I was staying with tried to find me a labouring job in a foundry. I started my first job in Smethwick as an unskilled labourer. The job was so appalling — dirt, heat and noise, the like I had never experienced. Within a week I left and wanted to go home. But it would have meant a great shame and embarrassment to my father and family. My next job was on the buses...as a bus conductor, as most Indian graduates ended up there.

Hero (1992: 320) describes the predicament of Indian and Pakistani teachers: 'Jobs on Bradford's local buses, however, remained the exclusive domain of highly educated Pakistani and Indians. A study in Coventry, reported in the *Morning Star* (5 January 1967), showed that half of the Indian bus conductors were university graduates'.

A lecturer in Education (male), formerly primary teacher, had a similar experience:

> I was a deputy head in a middle school in Punjab. On my arrival to this country I was advised by my friends to take my turban off. I refused. I tried for jobs in the factory; for teaching I had to do a fifteen's months course in this country. I became a labourer in a factory... One day my foreman told me — when he saw me reading the Guardian — don't waste your time here, try something else. So I started attending evening classes. I did a course in spoken English and later at the Nottingham University the course for overseas teachers. Then I got a job in a primary school...on probation for a year. I was a deputy head of a middle school in India with 9 years teaching experience, though.

A TESL teacher (male) described his experience:

> When I came, first I got admission in a linguistic course in Goldsmiths' College. I enrolled with the ILEA and an inspector interviewed me. He asked me to take elocution lessons and social skills training... Then I joined the industry, money was not enough... After that I spent sometimes in a school for a week to try out teaching. Students could be offensive and rebellious. I thought I must not plunge into it. I worked in industry for four months. Then I went to do a postgraduate course in English as a Foreign Language, part-time. Later I switched to full time... I had a grant. At that time accommodation was a real problem, and dearth of company.

Hero (1992: 119) summarised the situation extremely well when he wrote: 'Most of the bitterness expressed in the Asian community came from English-speaking and educationally qualified persons. And that too was mainly in the sphere of employment. They almost invariably found it a waste of time to follow up job advertisements in the newspapers and professional journals. Either no interview calls came or, when they did, British employers often treated their university degrees and professional experience as worthless. A typical experience was that of an Indian teacher in London who made nearly 300 applications but did not obtain a single interview. Not surprisingly, therefore, many qualified experienced teachers became bus conductors. A holder of MA and LLB degrees became a moulder in a Southall rubber factory; a police superintendent from Delhi, a machine operator... In Southall in 1966 there were nearly 1000 Indian and Pakistani university graduates, 84 percent of whom were engaged in semi-skilled, manual jobs... Of the 3500 Indian and Pakistani teachers who were issued B vouchers between 1965 and 1967 only a few hundred managed to find teaching posts.'

Taylor & Hegarty (1985: 518), in a comprehensive review of Asian children's education, make the same point by quoting relevant research: 'Even so, despite the absence of authoritative figures, it seems that relatively few obtained posts in the UK. For example, in a small scale study in 1967–8 out of 34 Indian and Pakistani male and female graduates who had previously been teachers or lecturers only three were teaching in UK, two after taking unskilled work initially'. Bagley (1969), analysing responses to a BBC programme, found that a large number of Indian and Pakistani immigrants had gained entry as qualified teachers on the B voucher system, but were unable to obtain teaching posts, even if they had been fortunate enough to undertake a short re-orientation course.

A special needs teacher (male) seemed to be quite bitter about his experience:

> To get a job in this country was one of the hardest thing. I applied 100 times. There were posters 'Come and teach in...'. When I went to see them, sorry we haven't got a job. These were the excuses. I started work in the post office. My wife joined me in 1963. ...One day I was standing outside the education office. Someone said to me: 'Are you applying for a teaching job?' I said: 'A Sikh gentleman MA, MEd with 10 years experience in a training college can't get a job because of his turban'. After a hard struggle I got a job...headmaster of my school had worked in the Indian Army; he was very co-operative.

In 1966, the DES instituted 4 pilot courses to cater for the needs of immigrant teachers. These were to be held at Nottingham University; Margaret MacMillan College of Education, Bradford; Whitelands College of Education, Putney; and Wolverhampton College of Education. These institutions were given a quota of 15–20 Asian teachers. They were to admit only those teachers whose qualifications had been recognised by the DES. Literature search showed only one published account of such a course (Brand, 1971). The course was to last for 15 months: one academic year for professional studies and one term for specialised English language teaching. According to Brand (1972: 146): 'The courses were quite deliberately designed to give a general training and the students were not encouraged to think of themselves as "Asian specialists"'.

The Nottingham course was oversubscribed in the year 1966. The tutors had little difficulty in selecting 18 Indian and Pakistani teachers, some with higher degrees. The objectives of the course were to improve the communication aspect of the spoken English and to re-orientate the students' attitudes to educational ideas and issues so that they could successfully practise in British schools. In addition, the course included teaching on the social structure of British society and its relationship to education. A primary school teacher (female), who took such a course, was full of praise:

> To begin with I was apprehensive, because I thought I had a master's degree and 8 years experience. But I then realised that my spoken English was not understood... I was not communicating. It was not only my English, but there was a wider problem of conversing with white colleagues and parents. I couldn't' understand them properly. I had no knowledge of the English system of education...the important provisions of the 1944 Act, for instance.

Nearly half the sample (12/25) had to undertake a course of further studies before they secured a teaching position. A home-school teacher (female) described her experience:

> I had a BA and BEd from the Punjab university, but it was not recognised for teaching in this country. I went to a college of education to do 2 years course... There was history of education, education psychology, and teaching methods. I also did teaching practice in local schools. (*Was it helpful?*) Yes, very much. I learnt a great deal, particularly improved my spoken English and learnt something about the local dialect.

A maths and science teacher (male), with a similar background to the above teacher, commented:

> My qualification was recognised for teaching, subject to verification from the Punjab university. The DES did not accept my degree testimonials, as there were rumours of forged degrees from India and Pakistan. When I got a temporary job in a science centre I was paid as an unqualified teacher at the rate of 37 shillings and 6 pence per hour. I got the job because there was a serious shortage of science teachers at that time (1959). There was no holiday pay. But my degree was not recognised equivalent to a British degree. It took the ministry some 8 months to verify my qualifications, then my pay was approximately £520 per annum. I joined the local university to improve my qualification. To improve my spoken English I started to have elocution lessons. At that time I realised how poor — different — I suppose my English was. I was also advised by my head to live in an environment where English was spoken all the time, as I was living in an Indian household

when I started teaching in 1959... There were only a handful of Asian teachers in the authority. I was completely at a loss. To tell you the truth I had no teaching experience and my 'practical' knowledge of science was abysmal, as we studied science mostly from books in my college. In the centre we were supposed to do practical work with the children. The classes were large, over 50 , and the kids couldn't understand my English and I couldn't understand theirs. It was absolutely hellish. I survived because of enormous help from my head. He was fantastic; invited me to his house, gave me advice on how to teach and plan my lessons.

Not all teachers had to struggle hard to obtain jobs. The head (female) of a school had it very easy:

My husband was already in this country, he got my DES papers ready. I came in March, 1963 and started teaching in September the same year. The job was in a primary/infant school. My English was good; I passed my probation in a year. I had an MA and 5 years teaching experience in India. I was district inspector there...I was hard working...I was welcomed in the school.

Likewise, a history and English teacher (male) got into teaching quite easily:

I had an MA in Persian and an MA in history and BEd with 8 and a half years experience in Pakistan. I got an interview for a teaching job without any difficulty. I was very much appreciated in the interview and got the job. There were no Asian or West Indian pupils at this school. It is a Roman Catholic school. I had no problems at all...the headmaster was very good. He helped me to settle down. There was a friendly atmosphere at school. I taught history from 1st form to 4th form and English to remedial classes. (*Any professional course in this country?*) No, the only course I did was BEd in Pakistan.

What emerged from the interviews is that the first-generation teachers who had good command of the English language and were from the urban background, predictably, did not have to face many difficulties in obtaining their first teaching post. However, teachers with 'language difficulties', who also tended to be from a rural background, met very many problems. Of that latter group of teachers, those with maths and/or science qualifications fared better; though most of them had to work, initially at any rate, in manual jobs and undertake a further course of study in the UK.

It is important now to discuss in some detail the major difficulty of the first-generation of Asian teachers: namely that of spoken and written English. This, according to our white interviewees, was the main problem in obtaining teaching posts and winning the respect and professional credibility of white colleagues.

An experienced white university lecturer (male) gave a lucid account:

> I have always regarded the command of the language to be paramount. I am particularly concerned with two areas: one would be teaching; and the other medicine. Because in both areas what is important is not what is going on on the surface, but the transaction between the clients. In the case of medical patients, who come to doctors and need assurance... The problem is of communication. How he/she describes the symptoms in accented, regional idiom and is not merely concerned to say how he/she is feeling in terms of latinate or international idioms, but that doctors and patients would be using the same language. I feel this also about teaching.

A white head teacher (female) described her experience:

> With Asian teachers it is the language: when I receive an application from an Asian teacher, I ring him/her up, ask a supplementary question. If I can't understand, I don't ask for references. Also many of them make elementary mistakes: head a letter incorrectly, do not sign off, or fill the rubric incorrectly. Then there are the usual; a few grammatical and spelling mistakes.

A white deputy head (female) put it more diplomatically:

> Yes, people like me couldn't understand them. We had to listen very hard. Children, though, got used to it. I even find it hard now to follow heavily accented English.

As regards the perceptions of our first-generation teachers, most of them (20/25) accepted this difficulty and tried to do something about it. A science teacher (male) narrated his experience:

> Yes, it is, and was, a dreadful handicap. It was so demoralising when white colleagues used to say: I beg your pardon, again, and again. Kids couldn't follow and I misunderstood their questions. Sometimes, a sympathetic child tried to so called 'translate' my English to the class. Particular difficulties were with the vowel sounds...v and w. It was not only the accent but the idiom as well; mannerisms and body language also come into play. Language is tied to one's culture — way of life, humour, jokes, folk tales and myths. My knowledge of the English society was based on Hardy and Shakespeare... It was very tough. I tried to give up many times and go back to bus conducting, but my headmaster persuaded me to hang on.

On the question of idiom, humour and comedy-hall jokes, a white lecturer (male) illustrated:

> Probably when teaching the native children, particular accent in a language which is alien to them is just funny. I know it sounds trivial that Peter Sellers' Indian-English had enormous effect on the British understanding and stereotypes, might even 'put downess' of Asian people. Sellars was one of the comic geniuses of the post-war period. He has done accents on Goons, etc. Sellers did the millionairess — it was undoubtedly funny. It is amusing as are some take-off of the Jewish accent.

Beryl Gilroy (1975: 163), a black teacher, vividly described an incident in her autobiographical account of her teaching experience in which a Bangladeshi teacher was involved. White teachers got very angry about this teacher's comments on the children's behaviour. They fumed: 'The bloody bastard — the bloody Pakistani nit, fumed May. Someone should do something about bastard like that, said Anne. Thank god for Peter Sellers — he takes liberties with them. Good luck to him. I feel like spitting at him, said another teacher. He's so bloody dogmatic'.

It seems to me Peter Sellers had a great effect in stereotyping the Asian accents as a comedy-hall joke.

The first-generation teachers mentioned many incidents where white teachers mocked their accent and mannerisms to amuse their colleagues in the staff room and sometimes mimicked Asian children's accent in the playground. This was considered to be a case of innocent humour. There were comedy shows in the 60s and 70s which also exploited the Asian accent and mannerism. The two most popular ones were: 'It Ain't Half Hot Mum'; and 'Mind Your Language'. A second-generation teacher (female) told me the following anecdote:

> We had several Asian teachers. They were all right — I used to find them quite funny really because the grammar was not as good as the other teachers' and their Peter Sellers' accent. (*Was it just English?*) This is what we were made to believe that the Asian people are not as good as the whites... Most of them taught maths and science.

A number of teachers almost develop an inferiority complex. Naseem Moolla (1991: 23), an Asian teacher, described her experience lucidly which is close to many teachers' perceptions: 'Many are the times I have received comments such as "don't you speak English well" or, "You speak and write English much better than me", as if some great compliment was being bestowed. I wish that on those particular occasions I could somehow let them take a peek at my self-concept to see what great chunks had been hacked off to make room for this amazing feat. A good command of "accentless" English and a wrench through the education system was not, alas, to prove to be my passport towards equality. The tragedy was that I expected them to be! Years of being subjected to processes of assimilation into British society had made me a guileless victim of racism.'

A TESL teacher (male) spoke eloquently:

> There were times when I disliked myself for being so inadequate in English. Despite my best efforts I couldn't change my accent. I stopped talking in Punjabi. I started disliking everything Indian. Our dress, food, marriage system, politics and religion appeared flawed to me. I shunned the company of Indian people. I tried to make friends with the whites. I tried to become what now a days is called a 'coconut' — black/brown from the outside and white from within. I feel ashamed of myself now. It was a period of serious crisis in my life.

A university lecturer (male), formerly a primary school teacher, argued:

> No doubt it is our second language and we haven't got the BBC accent, but our knowledge of the language is as good as the British teachers... Discipline depends on the school. If they control children they are called authoritarian. If we take the example of Eton or Harrow, it is authoritarian. Discipline is not a bad thing. English teachers lay emphasis on creativity, team teaching and the Open Plan. But when it comes to basic skills our teachers are OK... Children's attitudes can also be one of the reasons for poor discipline: some of them might think that Asian teachers belonged to an inferior race and not worthy of their respect.

Poor command of English has also been a major source of difficulty for Asian doctors in Britain. A research study on overseas doctors (Anwar & Ali, 1987: 62) dealt with the problem of communication of Asian doctors with patients. The following quote illustrates this well: 'But some overseas doctors admitted that sometimes there were language problems (one in ten overseas doctors mentioned this). An Asian consultant said: "Language problem — more of an accent and phrases". "The crux is good language, then (there is) no difficulty", explained another Asian consultant. One white doctor explained: "some are very good, some are awful...(relationship) not as good as with whites...language problems and ethical problems".'

Overseas doctors, since 1979, have to pass the Professional and Linguistic Assessment Board's language examination, even for temporary registration. There has been no such regulation concerning the recognition of overseas teachers' qualifications. Without doubt the poor command of written and spoken English caused a great many difficulties for the first-generation Asian teachers in their professional work and career enhancement.

Professional Difficulties

Interviewees were asked about their first impressions of white teachers, pupils and generally their perceptions of British schools. An account of a science teacher (male) is interesting:

> I was sent to a science centre on a temporary basis. This centre catered for the teaching of science to kids from the Roman Catholic schools in the city. It was right in the city centre…a grim place from the outside, anyway. I was to observe the head and other senior teachers for a month or so. I was impressed by the amount of science apparatus in the centre. There was a workshop for making equipment. Dedication of the teachers was impressive…they were there early, marking and preparing work for the children. Average class was around 50. In all lessons children were supposed to do practical work. Some of the experiments I saw I never did in my school or college days. So I have to learn from scratch.

Brand (1972: 151) also notes that the immigrant teachers were surprised to see the practical approach to science teaching as a normal part of class work in secondary schools.

A university lecturer (male) recounts:

> I was given a remedial class. I had no previous experience of this type of teaching. Also there was problem of communication — children found it hard to understand my English. I sought help from the headmaster. He was very good about it. He, so to speak, showed me the ropes. White teachers were polite and hard-working bunch, and after initial difficulties I enjoyed my teaching.

A primary school teacher (female) described her experience:

> My qualifications are from Kenya. I had Senior Cambridge Certificate and 2 years teacher training. I started teaching in 1966. I got my job on my first application. I was a deputy head in Kenya with 9 years experience, and here I was put on probation for a year. There were a lot of children from Muslim, Sikh and Hindu backgrounds. I suppose they needed somebody who could speak Punjabi and Urdu as most of the children spoke little English on entry. Now there are quite a few teachers from the ethnic background.

A maths teacher (male) recalled his difficulties:

> I got a job in a comprehensive school to teach mathematics. I got the

job because of my teaching subject. Headmaster was kind and settled me down. I did not know the modern methods of teaching. He kept helping me... Attitude of white colleagues? ...I thought it was OK then. But now I think there was a degree of paternalism there, in the sense that they didn't think my degree qualification was as good as their training college certificates. Not equality, by any means.

A primary head (male, first-generation) gave an account of his first impressions:

I did my post-graduate qualification in Edinburgh. I specialised in primary. I got my teaching post at the first go. It was in an all-white school, again at Edinburgh. I remember taking children to the park and people looking in amazement how a turbanned man can be in charge of white kids. I am, and was, a progressive teacher — worked hard. I enjoyed teaching maths, environmental science; jack of all trades.

Discipline

Discipline is one of the most troublesome areas for all the newly qualified teachers, particularly in secondary schools. Most of the first-generation Asian teachers in our sample found their first appointments in inner-city schools which were mostly attended by the 'poor whites' and the recently arrived Asian and West Indian immigrants. The staff turn-over in such schools was very high and the buildings uninviting and sometimes even rundown. A science teacher (male, first-generation) recounts:

I was very shocked to see the school building. It was right in the city centre. Traffic flowed on all sides. There was concrete hard ground for children to play. When I saw the children I couldn't believe I was in England. They looked so pale, poorly dressed, unwashed, unruly and rude. No school uniform, no ties. Absolutely shocking. Of course my imagery was based on the imperial projections of England, i.e. disciplined, rosy cheeked and well-mannered children...after all the battle of Waterloo was won on the play grounds of Eton. The headmaster was the only one who could control the classes. There was bedlam in other classrooms. Mind you, most were probationary teachers — yes, all whites. I was really scared. This didn't help matters.

Sikes, Measor and Woods (1985: 28) studied teachers' careers through the case study method. They write: 'Discipline maintenance seems to be the area which causes young teachers most anxiety'. They report a teacher's comment in some detail. Jan's (25, Scale 1, art) experience is typical: '...in this place they were all out to get me, the likes of the fourth years and the fifth years. I was new. And they do it with every new teacher I've since found out...they're just trying to see what reaction they'll get...did it with teachers when I was a kid'.

A secondary maths teacher (male, first-generation) had a similar experience:

> After passing my probation, I was sent to another school — a secondary modern. There I was given mostly junior classes and some work with the 4th and 5th years. I found it impossible to control the senior kids...they just did not accept my authority. They were trying it on. With the younger ones, I was more successful. But what appalled me was that most of them didn't carry any books, pencils, or pens. Everything was to be given out, counted, pencils sharpened, ink-wells filled, etc. and collected at the end. There was a chaos in the beginning and the end of lessons...sometimes most of the lesson was spent in giving out things. Coming from a strict and authoritarian educational background, I expected obedience and respect from the kids. (*Do you think there was an element of racism in it?*) No, I don't think so. I was not very confident and I suppose that came through. Also, communication was a big problem, though by now I was quite fluent; but it was not colloquial and the right idiom for kids. Most days I used to come home exhausted and think what have I accomplished today? Out of worry and anxiety I couldn't sleep. I had nightmares and dreaded Mondays. I wanted to leave teaching, but the head talked me out of it.

A secondary science teacher (female) also had nightmarish experiences:

> I had BSc first class and MA (Honours) in chemistry. I was given a temporary job in a large comprehensive school. To start with I used to wear a Sari...my language was all right but not good. One day, a boy came to me after the lesson and said: where I lived? I said why ? He said: 'I am going to come to your house and rip this thing off'. He was very abusive ...One day I will rip you out of our skin. He used to wear rings. Nobody took notice of it when I complained. I had difficulty in controlling classes. Inspectors came to check my teaching. They said: I should communicate with other colleagues.

This teacher had several other temporary appointments, but is at present teaching in a primary multicultural school. She feels happier in her job because she is contributing in a positive way to the Asian community.

Part of the difficulty arose from different perceptions and attitudes to learning, teaching and the nature of children. In Chapter 1, I described, in some detail, the research findings of a project designed to investigate the attitudes of Punjabi teachers to learning and teaching. The Punjabi trainee teachers scored significantly highly on five key items relating to children's ability, as compared with the equivalent British sample. These items were: some children ask too many questions; children are not mature enough to make their own decisions; children must be told exactly what to do and how to do it; a teacher seldom finds children enjoyable. From this research and literature survey it was argued that teachers in India tend to use rote learning methods to teach and that their relationships with students are formal and based on the traditional notion of respect for the teacher.

An experienced white headmaster tried to explain:

> Asian teachers engaged in teaching as second-language teachers — I am going back to early 70s — were very anxious to serve their community. They were mostly peripatetic and I think compared with this generation they were tentative. Partially they found the challenge difficult. They were strict and came from within a certain pedagogical tradition in which truth was articulated and handed down in ready-made packages. It was there to be received and absorbed by them without question. I did gain the impression in the 70s and early years, there was no critical tradition in Islam. But I have discovered in recent years that in higher education there is much more critical tradition within Islam than I had known. It does not reach down to schools in the same way as it does in the Western education, e.g. our teachers (brought up in the Western liberal tradition) would challenge pupil. To a degree it is true of the Muslim teachers and the Asian teachers. They have chosen subjects where that kind of thing is perpetuated: they choose science, maths. In these, the body of truth is fairly well-defined... I haven't met a geography teacher yet, but I am sure there are some around.

A senior white teacher (male) explained the situation at a more practical level:

> Maybe early difficulties were because many of them were not trained in this country and they came qualified from abroad, and obviously the major problem was the question of languageeThe other major difficulty to bring forth is their cultural differences:it is Ramadan. Then there was the problem of dress. Also their own value system played a part, which in a colonial sense is more to do with public school education and very much authoritarian and also the teacher should never be questioned. To my mind it is important to say things in group discussion; the Asian teachers were not used to it. In certain respects, these anecdotal narratives are in agreement with the research findings discussed in the first chapter.

A comment of a maths teacher (male) is revealing:

> This girl put her hand up to answer my question. She started saying: 'I think...' I thought how arrogant of this little girl of 12 to say I think. In

Punjabi society it is the collective which counts, more like we think or it is thought or the elders and teachers say, etc. Later on I realised that this is an important feature of the English education — to encourage independence of thinking. Same was the case with discipline: it was not that kids were undisciplined at that time, but inquisitive and lively. To manage classes in Britain one has to have a ready wit, tolerant attitude towards children and a very good grasp of the subject.

A university lecturer, former primary school teacher (male), also had a similar experience:

The only method I knew of teaching was class teaching: teacher dictating notes or giving sums for children to do. I was introduced to group work and child-centred education during my course in Notting-ham. I had no knowledge of other primary subjects, music, art and craft and PE. Also it was difficult to give my ideas a practical shape due to all sorts of reasons: a lot more preparation, changing my own attitudes about children, and class management.

A white head (female) made a different type of observation:

I had one Asian and one West Indian teacher... She (Asian) had a chapter of problems: wants to go back to India to meet her guru; she had a wedding to attend. Somebody has to teach her classes. Her arrogance was unbelievable; nothing given back. I find it difficult to understand. I am not a dragon, but it is difficult to get on.

This head is a personal friend of the researcher, but even then she asked me to turn off the recording cassette player and sought assurances that her identity would not be revealed. I realised from this incident how difficult it is to know the true views and feelings of persons in authority, especially on sensitive topics.

Brand (1972: 147), in a description of a course for the immigrant teachers, argued: 'It was clear that the two were inextricably linked and that as much of the immigrant's difficulty in communication could be attributed to what he was saying as it could to how he was saying it...the students' understanding of the primary and secondary stages of English education was confused and it was clear that the course would have to provide all students with opportunities of gaining experience of both stages'. The lecturer found that students were unfamiliar with important areas of the primary school curriculum: namely, music, drama, art and craft. Obviously such gaps in the knowledge of Asian teachers, in addition to their language difficulties, were probably the main reasons for the poor success rate in obtaining teaching posts in primary schools.

According to some teachers in the study Asians were given difficult classes. This resulted in poor discipline.

A teacher of special education (male) had an interesting observation to make:

> Discipline is no problem in primary schools for the Asian teachers. In secondary schools there is no support. They often teach in lower sets. Children there have family problems and social problems. All Asian teachers can't teach maths — they are given remedial classes.

Relationship With White Colleagues

I thought this was the most important aspect of teachers' experience to explore. Responses of the first-generation Asian teachers were mixed and varied. All the teachers, except one, agreed that their headmasters had been very helpful and supportive in their first teaching post. This may be due to the fact that the heads were prepared to accept an Asian teacher and were, therefore, morally obliged to provide a sympathetic environment. But relationships with white colleagues were problematic. A science teacher (female) had a particularly rough time:

> I wore a sari or a suit to work. They used to call me a Paki (*who?*), the white colleagues, or 'you coloured' etc. They would call me a Paki teacher...nobody used my name. Sometimes Madrasi curry and papadom. I used to take it. If you are a second-class citizen, you learn to live with it, otherwise you can't teach. My tension got worse, I couldn't swallow food... My male colleagues criticised my accent, my practical work and a lot of pressure was put on me.

This was an extreme case, but the other teachers also mentioned some difficulties with white colleagues. A science teacher (male, first-generation) recalled his first experiences:

> On the whole OK. But there were a couple of incidents which makes me think, now, that there was a hint of racism behind it. I sent a child out for being a nuisance. Within minutes he was back in my class. I asked: 'Why'. He replied that Mr. S... has asked him to go in and tell me that I have no right to send him out. Later on, he had to apologise, because the head took a firm stand. There was also a kind of condescending attitude — you are all right but not quite our equal. In a way coming from a 'colonial' background, I sort of accepted this attitude. Then there were racist jokes flying about in the staff room in the 60s ...A Pakistani was asked to carry a large package. He said: 'No, I only carry smallpox!' And I was supposed to laugh.

A primary head (female) made an interesting comment:

> In the beginning even young white teachers used to criticise my
> sentence construction. They used to say: 'She is doing the wrong thing'.
> I had the courage and self-confidence. So I went ahead in my own way
> — ignored the criticism.

A lecturer (male), previously primary teacher, was balanced in his criticism:

> Majority were sympathetic, and some had racist attitudes. But they
> came around. The head teacher was a racist — he thought Asian
> children are not very able and deserving only of remedial classes, but
> slowly he changed like other teachers.

A maths teacher (male) was very critical:

> I was not aware at that time, now I realise what they did to me. I am
> sort of late developer in this field. I was in this multicultural school with
> 90% Asian children without many Asian teachers, except one or two.
> Then I start feeling my presence was not welcomed. They didn't want
> me to be active — only want me to play the second fiddle. Something
> is wrong somewhere, I thought.

However, the senior white teachers thought relationships were good. A
white deputy head (male) ruminated:

> I must confess that I have never experienced it in those terms (i.e.
> problems between Asian and white colleagues). I couldn't imagine
> there could be a problem. In all my experience in eight schools in the
> inner city schools for 30 years, I felt that they were totally accepted. The
> misunderstandings related to methods of teaching and contents of the
> curriculum, which were outside their experience. In general, at staff
> room level, they were very well accepted.

A white head of a secondary school (male) gave a very measured and
balanced picture:

> The very first Asian teacher...was in a very large comprehensive
> school. A Sikh fellow; first he worked in the post office and then got a
> job to teach maths. He was very popular. He had winning ways. He
> related well, though he had difficulty with children. He had a heavy
> accent. He was hard work to follow... Children's attitudes were racist,
> but he coped very well... He wore his turban.

It seems to me that most of the first-generation Asian teachers had
problems, at least with some of their white colleagues. Some white teachers
felt superior to Asian teachers because of their British qualifications and the
fact that they could communicate with ease with children under their care.
Also some white teachers were, unintentionally and sometimes overtly,

racists. The Swann report (DES, 1985: 236) commissioned a research into the attitudes of teachers towards ethnic minorities in all-white schools. The researchers found: 'The whole gamut of racial misunderstandings and folk mythology was revealed, racial stereotypes were common and attitudes ranged from the unveiled hostility of a few , through the apathy of many and the condescension of others, to total acceptance and respect by a minority.'

Going Back

The intention of the majority of first-generation teachers was to improve their qualifications and to gain experience of the English education system with a view to going back to well-paid jobs at home. Most had this so-called 'five-year plan' to study and to work and then return to their home-lands. But only very few returned.

A teacher of community languages (male) explained:

> I came to this country in 1957. In India I was a teacher. I thought I would do a higher degree and gain experience and go back to a lecturing job, say in five years. My first job was in a factory, then on the buses as a conductor and later a trolley driver. At the same time I joined the university to study for Advanced Diploma in Education and then Master of Education. Time just went by — then I made another 5-year plan. I completed my PhD like this.

Anwar, in his book 'The Myth of Return' (Anwar, 1979), analysed the reasons for Pakistani immigrants seeking permanent residence in this country. Amongst the factors which he mentions to explain this situation is the economic and social uprooting from the country of origin. A story of a TESL teacher illustrates this:

> 'Go back', I said. What a difficult life. My white colleagues in the primary school used to criticise my work — I am not pulling my weight about discipline. Some would find fault with my craft work. I went to India for holidays and tried for a lectureship in English. There were hundreds of applicants for a single post. To get anywhere you have to have recommendations of a cabinet rank minister. I had lost my contacts during my several years stay in England. So I came back. It is not easy to re-establish yourself after leaving your country. People move on.

A maths teacher (male) had a similar story to tell:

> I was in this country for seven years. I had completed my MEd and gained experience in secondary schools. I thought I stood a good chance

of getting a job either in a good private school or a lectureship in a college. As a matter of fact one of my tutors gave me an address of a deputy head of a public school in Delhi, who wanted somebody with experience in England. Nothing came of it, I was never contacted. I must be honest; I only tried half-heatedly. There was so much nepotism — for buying a rail ticket you have to bribe, for getting your own money from a bank you have to wait and wait. I was fed-up. Despite all the problems in England, its pull was there: efficient public services, good facilities for travelling and personal freedom. Also I missed my friends. So I came back. I had no difficulty in getting a teaching job, though it was in the inner-ring area.

Second-Generation

The experience of the second-generation teachers is in marked contrast to that of the first-generation. In the first place, they had not to face problems which arise due to migration to a new country: namely, of personal and social adjustment; of seeking jobs and accommodation; and of trying to understand radically different social norms, family values and economic and political systems. Secondly, having gone through the British system of education, they had a good grasp of English and British institutions and the culture of the host society.

A primary teacher (female) reflected:

First-generation teachers found hard to get in — they needed polished top courses, I mean conversion courses. Their degrees were not recognised. Their language, not incorrect , but certainly very different in accent and vocabulary. I have done four years BEd course. (*Any language problem?*) No, I don't think so.

A senior secondary teacher science (male) amplified some of the points:

First-generation: can you imagine not being treated equal? Qualifications not recognised and language difficulties…they are real enough. When I first came to this school, a comment made was if you spoke on the phone, the listener would say you are an indigenous speaker of English. All my education is from this country.

However, a chemistry teacher (male), who came to this country at the age of 11, was not sure of his competence in English:

I was 11 years old when I came to this country and missed primary education. If I had come a year earlier and attended a primary school, my handicap would have disappeared. I spent a lot of time learning English. (*He had a slight Indian accent*).

There was one other second-generation teacher in the group, who came to Britain in his teens, and missed primary schooling and had a pronounced Indian accent. He was on a temporary basis and was thinking of leaving teaching. It is interesting to note that he was the only second-generation teacher who preferred to converse in Punjabi.

A science teacher (female) enlarged on some of the points:

> In my last school, this Asian teacher got the worst classes; he had discipline problems. He hadn't had promotion. He is waiting for the early retirement... A lot because of language. Also your expectations are totally different. If you have been to school in India you expect respect from kids — obedience. In a school like this, children argue back. You have to deal with it. It is difficult for your generation to accept that!

A secondary science teacher (female) recounted an interesting episode:

> My first contact with an India teacher...oh yes, his probation was extended. Because he was educated in India, they thought he couldn't handle the situation here. That was simply you can't trust the education system in India and their qualifications are bought, which to a certain extent is backed by facts. There was some corruption and bribery and cheating taking place somewhere in India. Another chap, first worked in a factory. Then he re-did his qualifications in the evening classes. He is a lecturer in a college in... A very determined person.

But another science teacher (male) was in a way unhappy about the poor professionalism of the first-generation teachers:

> I would be honest with you. First-generation teachers take ESL classes — OK. They are doing adequate jobs. They haven't gone through the system. Also language problem, as well. But sometimes I feel they have taken on something beyond their capacity; it undermines people who have full training. I want to make a success of this profession.

One second-generation primary teacher (female), whose father is also a teacher, was very complimentary to the older generation:

> To be quite honest, that generation had a better knowledge of the standard English than a lot of qualified teachers from this country. And in that sense, in the teaching of grammar, they were better qualified than myself and others. That was not the problem, I think. Maybe it was the actual accent. To some that might have caused problems...but then we have regional accents, Scottish and Welsh or Black Country. They had very little support from the family; the social expectations were different. They found it difficult to mix in with white colleagues;

they were not brought up here. We talk in the staff room, we share problems etc., and there are cultural aspects to all our discussions. Maybe they could not share these.

Most young teachers, though, expressed admiration and sympathy for the older generation for their determined efforts to make a success of their chosen career. But the 'language difficulties' and the authoritarian attitudes of the first-generation were often perceived to be the two major difficulties of the older generation.

First Appointment

Unlike the first-generation, the second-generation qualified teachers did not find any difficulty in obtaining their first post. Some were offered jobs, without formal application, by heads who felt that their schools needed ethnic minority teachers. Most of them applied to local education authorities in the 'pool appointment' category — the application is made to an authority rather than to individual schools. A teacher of modern languages (male) responded:

As it turned out they found me through the pool. I was happy to be there because of the mixture. I had my teaching practice in an all-Asian school, then I thought it would be good to be in a truly multicultural school.

A science teacher (male) explained:

I preferred to teach here because of Asian pupils. My first teaching practice was in nearly all-white school. There were a lot of single parents — considered to be a problem area. (*Did you have any discipline problems?*) Well, yes, I had problems. I did my second practice here and I was offered the job. I liked it from the beginning.

All second-generation teachers, except four, were teaching in multicultural schools. I thought it would be of interest to the reader to find out the possible explanation for this situation. A comment of an experienced white headmaster is revealing:

We had a Sikh maths teacher...there was an opportunity to move. The Sikh fellow — a very sensitive fellow — chose to go to outer-ring school. He was the only Asian teacher in an all-white school, and after about three months he came to see me. He encountered tremendous amount of prejudice and difficulty. Children openly challenged him in the class...coming around whilst he was teaching. Racial abuse, graffiti on the desk, the whole gambit. In all fairness to him, he chose to go to teach in a school which was very badly disciplined. I do know of other Asian teachers who coped better. A maths teacher went to an all 6th form college. So, no, it was very very difficult for him. I do know of Asian teachers who have chosen to go because they didn't want to be seen as the Asian teacher who could be a liaison teacher; the unofficial social worker in the school. Their perception of themselves was that of a professional teacher of their subject. Though they met a degree of prejudice, they managed to survive.

The whole tenor of the comment strongly implies that the Asian teacher's task in all-white schools is very onerous indeed, and only a few take up such a challenge. A deputy head (female) had a different angle to the problem:

They are first class role models, particularly the woman...she is not a Muslim. She is very traditional in her dress (wears Salwar Kamez), for instance. She can Speak Punjabi to them. (*Any language problem?*) No, not to the same extent (meaning as the first-generation). Again style is little abrupt. I don't how to explain? (*A bit authoritarian?*) Yes, that is what I mean. I would say: 'Go on do that please'. They would say: 'Go on do that'. It is far less obvious, though, in the second-generation.

A senior science teacher (male) gave an account of his experiences:

To a certain extent it is a destiny. It was a chance. I applied to...authority. They offered me a post. I have been here for 9 years. As you see it is a multicultural school and I like teaching here. I had quick promotions. (*Would you like to work in all-white school?*) I don't mind. As a matter of fact I am ready to make that move now; it could be any school. Perhaps, I have the gift of the gab. I haven't lost an interview yet.

This very tall Sikh teacher, with a turban and a beard, spoke in a BBC English accent and was extremely confident of his outstanding professional ability. He was convinced that things are going to turn out all right for him because of his thorough professionalism.

A head of infant school (female) had a ready explanation for her choice of school:

My catchment area is mainly Asian. A lot of mothers don't speak English...though second-generation is OK. I think I am helping the community in so many obvious ways. I understand Muslim parents' special problems and worries. I don't think a white person can do that.

A primary teacher (female) gave a more matter-of-fact reply:

I did one practice here, my last one. One in a white middle class school and the other one in a poor white school. I preferred this one. It is better organised and the children were treated better. There was a vacancy here, and I just applied for the job and got it.

The headmaster of this school is an Asian, who has forged good links with the ethnic minority parents (school is 95% Asians) and also has a clear policy on multicultural education including the teaching of community languages. Whether this was a contributory factor in her decision to teach in this school, it is hard to say. But, the head was keen to increase the number of ethnic minority teachers in his school in order to achieve a fair balance with white colleagues. This might also have played a part in her appointment.

All the second-generation teachers, except one, attended multicultural schools in England. This woman science teacher, who attended an all-white school, is presently teaching in an all-white school. She reflected:

> Most of my friends were English (her parents live in a middle class white area). To me relating to white kids and colleagues is no problem. I chose to go this school because it is near my home...I have no problems with white children or colleagues.

A modern languages teacher (male) explained his choice:

> As it turned out they found me through the pool. I was happy to accept because of the mixture (meaning the ethnic mix). I had taught, during my teaching practice, in an all-Asian school. (*What about all-white school?*) ...all-white schools, no, I am not sure whether I would feel comfortable. I am Asian/ black. How white students would view me? I will be worried about their attitudes.

Professional Difficulties: Relationship with White Colleagues

In sharp contrast to the first-generation teachers, the young teachers who had qualified from the British higher institutions mentioned fewer problems of adjustment. They were of the opinion that, as they have grown up with white people and understand their colleagues' attitudes and perceptions of Asian and black people, they can deal with arising tensions and anxieties. A science teacher (male) described his experience:

> In my first year I did not know how I was going to cope with the kids. You know how difficult things can be with a beard and turban (he had one himself). I thought if I can survive here, I would survive anywhere. I had trouble with tall boys. Once it went to the head. I was very apprehensive, but I coped. I have taken four assemblies and talked about Sikhism. I know whites' attitude; you got to mingle with them.

> The problem with the older generation was they kept themselves to themselves. They treat me very well indeed. There is a very strong socialist tradition in the LEA and it kind of all flows from there.

A chemistry teacher (female) described her experience:

> I grew up in an all white area. I went to an all white school and had white friends; therefore I am pretty much tuned to the system. My predecessor came from India...a very large chap and apparently he was totally unsuccessful. He had a language problem: his accent was very pronounced. There are rough kids in the school. They were totally out of control with him. We have six Asian teachers; one or two are very good. They don't have the relationship, good relationships, I mean.

A woman primary school teacher, working in a multicultural school, described how the white staff value Asian teachers' contribution:

> White colleagues often chat to us at lunch about our religion, family or whatever. They ask, what does it mean? And we translate the meanings of the symbols. Basically, you share your knowledge. So white colleagues appreciate our help. In this school it is very good, because we have a young staff. All is new to them and they are keen to learn.

Another woman primary teacher was cautious in her comments:

> I feel, certainly old generation have suffered quite a lot. They worked as hard as they could...they have been exploited. Put upon a lot. But their work was not recognised. With us, not to the same level. White colleagues make certain assumptions about us, Asians — even stereotyping. This white teacher kept on kissing my hand every time he saw me. Half of me thought it was out of respect and the other half thought he was taking the mickey out of me. And, then, invariably some white colleagues ask personal questions about my arranged marriage. (*What about professional matters?*). Yes, there is no problem at that level. In promotion it may be a different story.

Concluding Remarks

There are several points emerging from the interview data. Firstly, the difficulties faced by the first-generation teachers in schools were mainly due to the 'language problem'. This was pointed out by the senior white teachers and lecturers, and the majority of the Asian teachers in the study also accepted this shortcoming. The related problem of the first-generation's traditional attitude to children and their learning is less transparent but, nevertheless, is an important factor in building up relationships with pupils and in actual classroom teaching. This factor was further compounded by the lack of first-hand experience and deep knowledge of the British system of education and way of life.

Secondly, the first-generation's knowledge of academic subjects was mainly acquired through formal book learning and presented difficulties with practical demonstration work in the classrooms.

Thirdly, the attitudes of white colleagues to the new Commonwealth teachers were somewhat condescending, if not downright racist (see DES, 1985). As a result, it seems to me, an atmosphere of tension and anxiety prevailed in some multicultural schools. In a few it led to the alienation of first-generation Asian teachers.

Lastly, it became clear from the interviews that the second-generation teachers do not face the same problems as encountered by the older generation. Though the majority have preferred to work in multicultural schools, they have not found relationships with white colleagues or students as problematic. They found no difficulty, whatsoever, in getting their first appointment. Whether they will continue to have a smooth passage is a matter of some conjecture, but they certainly have made a very good start.

3 Life in School : Multicultural Issues and Concerns

This chapter deals with the professional issues relating to multicultural education. These involve the teaching of community languages; Eurocentric curriculum; achievement patterns of Asian and Afro-Caribbean students; young peoples' identities and biculturalism; home-school links; separate schools; gender issues; equality of opportunity; racism in schools; participation in their community's affairs; and the future of race relations in Britain.

The method used to collect information was described in detail in Chapter 1. Briefly, it consists of gathering information through in-depth interviews which are semi-structured. The emphasis is on exploring the interviewee's perceptions of events as he/she construes them. I fully agree with the sentiments of Zec (1993: 231) who asserts: 'It has become widely accepted that, in seeking to understand a social situation, it is essential to listen to how its actors describe it, and their position in it'. The usual criteria of reliability and validity, in the strictest sense, is not applicable to this kind of research as the major purpose of such inquiries is illuminative rather than confirmatory.

In order to understand the dynamics of inter-cultural encounters during the passage of time, i.e. from the early 60s until the present, the narrative at all stages embraces the comparison of perceptions of two generations of Asian teachers.

Community Languages

The teaching of community languages has been a contentious issue. Asian parents have been divided on how best to preserve their language and at the same time not to disadvantage their children at school. In the 50s and 60s, the prevailing attitudes of the majority of white teachers was that the learning of a minority language takes up useful time which could be devoted to the learning and mastery of English. A teacher of community languages (male, first-generation) explained:

> It has gone through several phases; in the 50s the main emphasis was on the teaching of English in schools. No attempt was made to do anything about minority cultures and languages. The shift came about in the late 70s — but then it was to do with the European languages. I think it was the early 80s when the minority languages were considered. It was a welcome sign. Asian children began to feel important about their own culture.

A teacher of maths (male, first-generation) told me an interesting story:

> I recall in the mid-60s my sister's children came to the UK to join their father, who came in 1960 and was a bus driver — though he was a teacher in Punjab. Anyway, the kids couldn't speak much English. We started a big drive to teach them English. They were told off for speaking Punjabi with one another and with the elders, except with their grandmother and mother. We thought somehow Punjabi will interfere with the learning of English — that was the wisdom of the time. At any rate Punjabi was, and regrettably still is, considered to be a low status language in India — Hindi is more prestigious and English speakers are thought to belong to the elite class. So there were all sorts of misguided reasons for abandoning Punjabi. Now they don't speak Punjabi at all. And they can't read nor write. We all have come to regret this.

It is interesting to compare this situation with that of Wales. In the 40s and 50s, there were many Welsh parents who were led to believe that their children would be at a disadvantage if they were to learn Welsh and to become bilingual. This was based on the conception that the brain has a limited capacity for learning and information processing. Bellin (1995) states that it is based *on the worry that having too many languages would somehow take up capacity or 'room' and have less capacity for education generally.*

There are several teachers of both generations who expressed reservation, on practical grounds, about the issue of teaching community languages.

A university lecturer (male, first-generation) argued:

> …Yes, should learn it. But which one? Urdu, Punjabi, Gujarati, etc. No harm in teaching. Again you must have qualified teachers. Our generation can't speak English fluently…it is a very big problem.

A white headmaster (first-generation) had similar reservations:

> What these kids (meaning Asians) need is more practice in English not

in Urdu. They ought to speak English at home, listen to the radio and read English books. This is the only way they can achieve higher academic standards. They might have a reasonable command of the spoken English, but they need to work at their written English. (*What about community languages?*) We have classes in Urdu and Bengali and they are reasonably well attended.

An Asian headmaster of a primary school (first-generation) gave a realistic picture:

Community languages are taught after school. I have three classes a week. Sometimes it bulges and other times it goes down. In summer they want to go home. There is a core (of parents) who are very interested. Majority are not bothered, only a small core and the professionals. If you talk to the parents, they say we want our kids to achieve; that is it. If they learn Punjabi it is OK, but they are not insistent, not pushing. But given the circumstances it is sometimes difficult. We have difficulty in our own family. My own kids can't read or write Punjabi. They were never given the opportunity. Now I make a point of speaking in Punjabi, but they respond in English. They can speak if forced to. It is tough.

A senior teacher (female, second-generation) expressed her predicament in a similar way:

My kids go to a private school. The headmaster there thinks traditional discipline is good for the children. (*Can they speak and read Punjabi?*) No, my son and daughter can't read or write Punjabi. My daughter is starting now. I have a friend who teaches her and then I do a bit extra. We just go through the same work again. My son is already doing three languages (French, Greek and Latin) at school; it is too late for him. So I don't want to put extra pressure on him at this stage. He can pick it up later. We speak Punjabi at home with our parents.

A primary teacher (female, second-generation) also gave a personal account:

I am making a conscious effort with my daughter. She is 5. She finds it very difficult to communicate in Punjabi — we have to say to her constantly to answer in Punjabi. That purely is our own fault, because we communicate in English. Why are we speaking English all the time?

A science teacher (female, second-generation) also felt guilty about the situation:

Language is a way to literature. It is unfortunate we are losing it. I don't think it is intentional. It is a shame. It is terribly unfortunate that I don't feel comfortable with my own language. My son understands Punjabi (he goes to a public school)...what I found is that children who speak Punjabi stop by the age of 11 or 12, anyway. (*Reason?*) They feel ashamed of their own language. I would be happy to send my son to a community school if it were outside the '*Gurudwara*'. The community languages are being recognised alongside the modern languages, they used to be after school. But it should be built into the curriculum, that's where its place is. It should be offered to non-Asians as well.

However, some second-generation teachers are quite determined to maintain their mother-tongue. A primary teacher (female, second-generation) was committed:

I speak Punjabi at home. She (her daughter) understands more Punjabi than English. Well, this is the way I want it. I want her to grow up reading and writing Punjabi. I would encourage, because I missed out on that one...my husband can write, but I cannot.

A TESL teacher (female, second-generation) had a different angle on the issue:

Yes, it should be taught — personally I feel it's parents' obligation; speak and make an effort. You have to make a decision in a school where there are six languages: what I am saying is, it's pace is generally in the home. Anyway, the Section 11 funding (special fund from the DES instituted in 1966 to help inner-city schools) now would support only the teaching of English as a second language. There won't be any money for the mother-tongue teaching.

Generally, there was a stronger support from the first-generation teachers for the maintenance of the mother-tongue. A teacher of community languages (male, first-generation) expressed his views forcefully:

Yes, its place is in the curriculum. After a brief spurt, it is being reduced. I am worried. Community languages would be finished. In the schools, community languages have no status at all. Generally speaking, white teachers regard it as second-rate.

However, most second-generation teachers were also committed to the teaching of community languages. A modern languages teacher (male, second-generation) argued:

Yes, very definitely. From my own experience I can say it would be a great advantage. If I can offer Hindi or Punjabi as well as French and Spanish — another string to your bow. Language is tied to one's identity and culture, that is why I think it is so important; helps us to root ourselves.

Likewise a teacher of modern languages (male, second-generation) commented:

> Oh, yes. It is very important indeed, I had no opportunity to do Gujarati which is my native tongue. When I went to the grammar school I had so much work, I hadn't the opportunity to follow it up. I can speak, but can't read or write. This is true of lot of us...I have lost out on the ability to communicate with friends, relatives and also lost my part of identity and culture. I think it should be part of the school curriculum.

A PE teacher (male, second-generation) opined:

> Religious and social identity of our people is tied to our language. I have been talking to *Pushtu* speakers. They feel they have lost out...I want community languages to be very much part of the school curriculum.

All the Asian teachers, both of the first and the second generation, were convinced of the value of teaching the community languages. Languages are considered to be the key elements of ethnic minorities' religion and culture. But 1 first-generation and 4 second-generation Asian teachers were not in favour of including them in the school curriculum owing to practical difficulties.

A white university lecturer (male, second-generation) summarised this dilemma:

> Given the best will in the world — ignoring our limited resources — I can't see how you could adequately provide for courses in Bengali, Punjabi, Hindi etc. where the majority and a significant minority share a language, yes, I do think so. But unfortunately my judgment is becoming clouded by the National Curriculum: children have to do 10 subjects. Maybe it is asking too much of children. As regards European languages, part of me says: it is excellent. Part of me says: learn the mother-tongue. We are faced with a paradox: in order to provide further and deepen cultural experiences by teaching community languages, you are denying them chance to learn a European language. Britain is linked to Europe now. There are certain types of jobs which require Spanish or German.

In my recent research with Asian young people, parents and community leaders, I found that the majority of respondents would like the community languages to be part of the school curriculum (Ghuman, 1993). However, the issue of teaching community languages is a contentious one. On the one hand, there are educationalists (Cummins, 1988; Skutnabb-Kangas, 1988; Tosi, 1988; Bourne, 1989) who are convinced of the educational, cultural and social benefits of enlightened bilingual/multilingual policies for all schools. On the other hand, there are some parents, teachers and liberal academics who, on purely pragmatic grounds, favour ethnic communities being responsible for the teaching of their own languages and culture (see Rex, 1985).

Cummings (1988) argues that it is imperative that minority students' languages and cultures are included in the school curriculum and that the teaching methods promote an interactionist stance in which students actively participate with their linguistic and cultural experiences. Such a policy would be based on the notion that bilingualism is an additive experience. Skutnabb-Kangas (1988) believes in the 'enrichment theories', and argues that the child's mother-tongue should be a positive starting-point for the school. Bourne (1989) carried out a comprehensive study of 'Education Provision for Bilingual Pupils' in England and Wales. The study is wide-ranging and rich in details on policy and the provision of English language teaching, community languages and bilingual support. She urges practitioners and others to learn from the Welsh experience and to promote a bilingual perspective in schools, which should enhance the cognitive development and cultural enrichment of all pupils. Steiner-Khamsi (1990) argues that the recent 1988 Education Reform Act leaves the issues of community languages untouched; if anything it further marginalises them and leaves them to the idiosyncratic policies of LEA s and schools.

On the opposite side of this debate are some Asian parents, white teachers (see Ghuman, 1993) and some academics (Stones, 1980; Rex, 1985) who believe that in the present political climate schools ought to concentrate on enabling ethnic students to gain good academic and vocational qualifications so that they can compete with their white peers to some advantage. Also, it is felt that the available resources should be used to teach English so that children can become fully competent in the language of the host society.

The Asian communities are deeply divided along the lines of religious, caste and regional affiliations. There is no united movement by Asian parents to advance the cause of community languages in schools. For instance, Punjabi-speaking Hindus and Muslims want their children to learn Hindi and Urdu respectively, and not Punjabi as this is deemed to be the language of the Sikhs. In reviewing the bilingual situation in Wales, Bourne comments (1989: 19): 'It requires an act of will for minority communities to retain and pass on their languages and cultures, and this commitment must be a crucial factor in encouraging young people to choose teaching as a profession'.

The Muslim community in Britain is better organised for such a collective action as compared to the other Asian communities. *The Observer* (2 August, 1992: 2) reported: 'There are more than 21 full-time private Muslim schools in Britain and these schools will apply to opt-in to the state sector. This has been accomplished through a well-organised campaign by the Muslim Education Coordinating Committee, UK'.

There is another dimension, however, to the teaching of community languages. The vast majority of the ethnic-minority language teachers were, and are, of the first-generation. There is a serious shortage of qualified second-generation bilingual teachers to implement even the most modest programme of community language teaching in Britain. Ideally, of course, if it is planned to preserve the minority languages, we need bilingual schools as in Wales (Baker, 1985). But this will remain a distant goal in Britain for the foreseeable future, given the present government's lack of policies on multicultural and bilingual education.

Euro-centric Curriculum

Teachers' opinions were sought on whether the school curriculum has changed following the recommendations of the Swann committee (DES, 1985) and other advisory bodies (e.g. Schools Council Report, 1981; Rampton Report, 1981) which have advocated the inclusion of multicultural material and intercultural perspectives in the school curriculum. All the Asian teachers in the study thought that the changes have been mainly cosmetic and peripheral. A comment of a TESL teacher (female, second-generation) illustrates this:

> White teachers still make certain assumptions…this teacher asked an Indian girl how do you make tea at home. The girl said: 'you take a saucepan…' The teacher interrupted: you don't need a saucepan for that. This is a simple example, but shows how a child's experience is ignored. You call it ethno-centricism…one's own way of doing things is the best, I think! So if you don't make tea the English way you are not civilised. …Children begin to dislike their own ways. Multicultural curriculum is more important for the whites. But it is very difficult to address this in a practical way.

A white head of a multicultural primary school (not in the sample studied) admitted quite frankly:

> The content of the curriculum has not changed. Our curriculum is the same as in the outer-ring area. But our delivery of it is different. Parents want good level of achievements and they leave it to us to achieve it.

All Asian teachers felt that it is equally important for all-white schools to have a multicultural dimension. A teacher of Urdu (male, second-generation) made this suggestion:

> White children and teachers should know about our culture...enjoy our food and dress; know religion and history. It is only happening in some black schools — it should be in all schools.

A white TESL teacher (female, second-generation) observed:

> I am not an idealist as I used to be...it is not widespread, it should be. Reality is different. You would have thought it would be the norm. It all depends on particular schools. Changes are not even tokenistic in some places. I find it quite depressing.

A large number of Asian teachers (44/50) in the study took the view that multicultural education means a good education and should not be considered as a separate subject. A home-school link teacher (female, second-generation) observed:

> We should use the experience which children bring into the school. This is supposed to be an important psychological principle which is the basis of sound classroom practice.

A white secondary head (female, first-generation) argued that she had made a number of changes in her school:

> We have cleared the books which were racists and also sexists. We have turned it on its head. We have introduced elements of world history. We have ordered a lot of tapes, books, charts and other relevant material for the library. A number of staff has been on in-service courses.

As regards their own contribution to this educational policy and practice, Asian teachers made several sound proposals, but also expressed cynicism.

A TESL teacher (male, first-generation) argued:

> Most schools in B ...have a good source for teaching inter-cultural understanding. There are teachers from various religious backgrounds and cultures who could take morning assemblies and advise white teachers. But this is not utilised. Some white teachers do a year's course in multicultural education and think they have become experts in all aspects. I had this white woman teacher arguing with me that India has hundreds of languages; which one do we choose to teach...also for many whites this has become another way of gaining promotion. Many ethnic teachers are left out in the cold.

An Afro-Caribbean maths teacher (male, first-generation) also expressed his doubts on his school's policy:

> No, they are encouraged to speak Standard English, in fact. Creole is not recognised as a language — no exam like in Urdu. If we are a multicultural society, this has to be tolerated. They pay lip service in schools, but very little gets done. Part of the curriculum, 4 hours, are devoted to general Black Studies, only for Jamaican children. This should be for all the children. 1066 and all that, what is it to me? I didn't know my own culture. Our books were English orientated and our community did not get a look in.

An Afro-Caribbean RE teacher (male, second-generation) commented on the positive aspects of having children from different religious backgrounds:

> I have Hindus, Buddhists, Christian and Muslims in my classes. I had to learn a lot from the pupils and read a lot...to be able to understand what the different faiths have to say. For example, Hinduism have many gods, what have they got to say? They do believe there is one God, but many facets. I try to draw strands from different religions. Say, Muslims go to Mecca for Haj. They wear Haj clothes, take shoes off. It is different, but not silly.

A white deputy-head (male, first-generation) felt slightly embarrassed by the way Asian teachers were used, or exploited:

> In management terms, some said how can we use them? They translated, met parents and acted as secretaries — I mean general dogsbodies. That is not good enough now... But you must understand the vast majority of white schools have no conception of multicultural education — as a matter of fact it is more important for them than us. We have to live it. There is no choice for us. I had a daughter in an all-white school; an Asian child came to the same class. No white child would sit next to her. In the early days class looked side-ways. Who was going to be friends with her? There was enormous confusion. It is a middle-class area. Even in 1990, it was considered to be a problem.

A white head teacher (male, first-generation) had a very positive image of the Asian teachers' contribution:

> I recall my experience of Asian teachers engaged in teaching as a second language. I am going back to the early 70s. They were very anxious to serve their community. They were mostly peripatetic and very well-received in their schools. But I met them because we were developing an RE syllabus. They enhanced my understanding of Islam

and Hinduism. I think compared with this generation there was a marked lack of confidence. At that stage they had doubts about their role. They were very tentative; partly they found the challenge difficult. They emphasised commonality rather than differences. The current generation is different. They are supportive (i.e. of multicultural initiative), but not aggressively so. Muslim teachers are willing to help in the morning assembly...but not to recruit children for the Mosque.

The crucial problem of curriculum innovation, particularly in all-white schools, remains unresolved. The 1988 Education Reform Act has made the bad situation even worse. The overt and covert attitudes of successive education ministers have been downright hostile to any form of multi-cultural education (see Verma, 1992: 13–16). Furthermore, inner-city schools are becoming 'monoethnic' minority schools. On the other hand, outer-ring schools in most cities are mostly all-white. Thus we see the polarisation of schools along ethnic groupings, which cannot be conducive to the development of a tolerant multicultural society.

Education of Asian Children and Young People

All the teachers in the study were asked questions relating to the educational progress of Asian children and young people. The first important topic discussed was their level of achievement as compared to their white and black peers.

The majority of the Asian teachers (39/50) felt that the achievement level of Asian students ranges from average to above average. However, some teachers were sceptical. In their view, the performance level of Asian-origin students is often compared with that of the white inner-city students, who also tend to have a lower socio-economic background. The correct comparison should be with that of a representative sample of white peers, including those of middle-class.

A lecturer in education (male, first-generation) argued:

It is difficult to say — but their potential is not being realised; this is my observation. Some of the reasons are: working in English, which is their second language; low expectations of teachers...some white teachers mock their (students') high expectations and treat them badly.

A home–school liaison teacher (female, first-generation) described her experiences:

Low expectation is the chief cause of low attainment...I give you an example: A young 5-year-old Muslim child was thought to have no language at all! She was left alone by the teacher for a year. Then one day whilst she was playing in a Wendy house, she was being bullied by a white boy. Suddenly she gave him a torrent of abuse: f— off and the like. The teacher was amazed: she thought because this child is wearing Pakistani clothes she won't have any English. (*What about the young teachers?*) They are all right to start with but get sucked into the prevailing 'staff-room' culture.

There is some evidence to support this contention. Troyna (1991: 373) reports the findings of his small-scale ethnographic research which indicate how the self-fulfilling prophecy of low expectations is realised. He concludes: 'The evidence presented in this article provides clear-cut evidence of the way Asian pupils, at the time of study, were denied equality of opportunity in the school... First, on their entry to Jayleigh Asian pupils tended to be assigned to learning groups in English and mathematics that were below their ability levels as assessed by their primary groups. Second, the implications of this misallocation were profound... The relatively lower number of Asian entrants into the GCSE examinations in year 5 can only be understood and explained in relation to the internal processes of allocation and selection which the school operated.' An earlier study by Wright (1987) showed a similar predicament of Afro-Caribbean students in a comprehensive school.

An Afro-Caribbean teacher (male, second-generation) gave a personal account of his own schooling which gives a degree of support to the 'low expectation syndrome':

I came in 1955, one of the originals, you know. I started school but did not succeed. I don't know why? I think the indication I had was that I was not working hard...but at that stage I vowed to work hard. Then I was sent down a class, where kids just messed about. That's where my life began to be lost, really. It could be my fault or could be stereotyping by the teachers.

A white secondary head (female, first-generation) gave a very factual account:

We have lifted our tail, but not our head. Only 14% get pass grade at the GCSE examination. White boys achieve the best and the least, black girls do better than black boys and the Asian sample is too small to generalise.

A secondary head (female, first-generation) was very candid in her observation:

Achievement levels are mixed. In inner-city areas, teachers are not of good quality...they go in the inner-circle schools when they can't find promotion in the outer-circle schools. Then, there are discipline problems — attitudes are negative. But there are some kids who do achieve.

A well-researched report by Smith & Tomlinson (1989) shows that the performance of Asian students, with the exception of Bangladeshis, is very close to that of the white students when social class and other relative variables are taken into account. However, in the inner-city schools, Asian students, again with the exception of Bangladeshis, have generally performed better than the whites. *The Independent* (8 March, 1990) summarised the Inner London Education Authority's (ILEA, now defunct) report with a bold headline: 'Indian children best performance in school exams'. The paper goes on to describe the main reason: 'Indian families put pressure on their children to succeed and teachers had high expectation of them'.

However, blanket judgments of this nature might have to be qualified in the light of research evidence. There are variations in educational aspirations and attitude to education among the Asian community in Britain. A recent report of the Policy Studies Institute (Jones, 1993: 151), on the position of ethnic minorities in the mainstream British society, concludes its findings as follows: 'The findings suggest that the south Asian population contains both the most and the least successful of ethnic minority groups that we have studied. At one extreme we have the African Asian and Indian populations. These groups have higher proportions of well-qualified people, have attained comparable (or better) job levels to whites, and have unemployment rates closest to those found among the white population. At the opposite end of the spectrum there are the Pakistani and the Bangladeshis. They retain the largest proportion, even among young people, with no formal qualifications of any ethnic groups. They have substantially lower job levels than people of other origins, and consistently suffer the highest rates of unemployment.'

The report further draws our attention to the significant differences which exist among the Asians in scholastic achievement levels and that of economic performance. The reasons for these differential performances are complex, but one of the factors is the potency of home culture to the motivation and the will to succeed. In California, Gibson (1988: 171–2), explaining the superior performance of Punjabi Sikh students over that of white students, came to the following conclusion: 'Asian Americans are said to do well academically, in part at least, because of cultural traditions that promote success in school. Such a case may certainly be made for Valleyside Punjabis. Cultural and religious values, together with the particular nature of the Valleyside setting, help Sikhs adapt to the demands of their new environment and overcome many of the hardships they encounter in school.'

Competence in English

The majority of Asian teachers (42/50), of both generations, thought that children who were born in Britain, and have been to a play group and attended a nursery, are better prepared to learn English in the Infant and Primary schools. An Asian primary head teacher (male, first-generation) explained the situation:

> Two or three things about Asian kids coming to school — I don't want to sound snobbish or bigoted — but children come from different classes and castes. Children come with all sort of disadvantages; social, economic and financial. As for English, they come with little English. But I wouldn't call it a disadvantage. This is my personal opinion. But it is the poor experiences which are a problem — the family background and parents' outlook. Those who were born here and have gone through the system, their language is generally very good.

An Asian head of infant school (female, second-generation) gave an account based on her experience:

> With some children there is a problem. All depends on the socio-economic groupings they come from. Of course parental interest counts as well. Also if they have older brothers and sisters who can speak English. By the time they go on to a primary school their English is quite good.

However, there were reservations from the secondary teachers. A white (male, second-generation) secondary teacher explained:

> They all communicate very well, but there is a distinct advantage to black and white children. They can use idioms and have richer vocabulary than Muslim kids. Even if they (meaning black and white) are not bright, they can use metaphors, idioms with ease. For instance, kids in my class did not know 'thigh'— they have a restricted vocabulary. Even when the kids were born here. English is still not their first language. Of course, a lot depends on the home-background. If a family is English-speaking, it is alright.

Likewise a white TESL primary teacher (female, second-generation) expressed her doubts:

> Children who were born here...quite a few are with very little English. It seems to vary a lot: 5th form girls were amazingly bad... That they have been through the system and they were born here. I was quite

shocked, really. They have not been picked up. They communicate so well orally, but in their written work it was disastrous.

A white deputy head of a secondary school (female, first-generation) gave a factual account which is based on her own school:

English is affected a stage earlier. They don't learn at the nursery stage or even earlier. If they are good, they are 2 years behind when they enter our first form. About 30 out of 210 are very basic — may be 5 years old reading level. (*Were they born in this country?*) Oh yes.

A white teacher in charge of a TESL unit in a predominantly Asian (Muslim) school thought that 80% of children in the school needed some form of language support. It is difficult to verify this fact but, obviously, if it is true, it is a serious cause for concern.

Gender Issues

The main concern of teachers and others is that Asian parents, in general, do not allow the same degree of personal freedom and equality of opportunity to their girls as they do to the boys. Almost all the teachers expressed their concern over 'inequality' between boys and girls, but related it to the social conventions and cultural imperatives of the Asian communities.

A primary teacher (female, first-generation) explained:

Parents are very strict. Second-generation girls suffer the most. Parents have double standards — one for the boys and another for the girls. They say it is part of their culture. When the girls come home, they have to change into Indian costumes. They are not allowed to go out. Boys can even have girl-friends. But a lot depends on the family.

A secondary teacher (female, first-generation) had a different angle on the problem:

Dating is going on all the time. During my days it was more clandestine, but they are far more open about it. Even now when boys date, it is generally accepted. But, definitely, unacceptable if girls do. Our religion and culture tolerate this inequality. Gender inequality gets me. It is everywhere. They say: 'she is a bad girl, because she has split the family'; and 'she is a lovely girl because she has united the family'. ... I don't need a man to look after me. I am sick of hearing this from other women. A lot of educated girls are going away from our culture. They are sick of being treated as second-class citizens.

Another secondary teacher (female, first-generation) made similar observations:

I watch girls at lunch time; they pull up their long skirts, loosen their hair and put lipstick on. They are transformed. Some of them have boy friends — others like to look attractive. I see a lot of Asian young men at lunch-time and home-time around school...they (girls) often pick up the worst aspects of European culture and look cheap.

A TEFL secondary teacher (male, second-generation) made some additional points:

There are some traditional things with girls. Girls should help their mothers with the house work...all girls find a lot of problems: especially Muslim girls. I lost 2 or 3 girls from my sixth form, they said they are needed at home. Some parents don't want their daughters to study after the age of 16. They are sent to Pakistan. There is no need for that. They have worked hard during their school life to get good grades. We are told that their relatives are not too well and need help. It is difficult to find out the truth.

A white deputy head of a secondary school (male, second-generation) thought that the majority of girls come to accept double standards:

Yes, girls have less freedom. The girls cope well in school and majority accept that home is different. I took 9a to see King Lear. This father won't let his daughter go. We are finding the parents approach us about their anxieties. We assure them that they (girls) would be safe, then they are more willing. But not on residential weekends; very very few of them would let them. ...Mums think we might give them the wrong food, or they might wear shorts and their husbands might see them. Mothers are torn between what they can do for their daughters, and husbands finding about it. Slowly, more and more girls are staying for further education. When they see their peers doing well — but still a long way to go. With boys there is no problem. They have so much more freedom. Sons are allowed to do what they want to do. They are not firmly disciplined. But I must say women are quite dominant in the home... They are quite strong in a lot of cases.

A teacher of modern languages (male, second-generation) confirmed what was described by the white deputy head:

...Very definitely, I can give you a number of friends who were with me in the sixth form, who had better grades than me are now married with children. At the age of 18 their fathers said no. Young girls are becoming strong now. They are saying: 'stop us if you dare, this is the last time you would speak to me'. I am not saying they are happy, but 10 years ago no. Parents are now beginning to compromise...my sister met a man. He was at M...university. They had secret meetings. My mother knew. My dad was not happy because the village, in Punjab, which his family came from was not that big (meaning insignificant)!

A secondary science teacher (male, second-generation) explained how some girls can lose motivation as a result of parents' negative attitude to girls' education:

> Girls are not very responsive; boys are very boisterous. You have to push them (girls) real hard. Motivation is not very good. Some are sent back to Pakistan and Bangladesh to go and get married there to a relative. So girls say why bother.

A white head teacher (male, first-generation) narrated an event which highlights some of the difficulties:

> We have two classic cases. In one case the father would not let her (daughter) work within the area. So I paid for her 'A' level correspondence course. She ran away from home to go to London to study law. The family caught up with her, as they always do — the network is amazingly good. They took her to her brother's house... The police said to the girl we can take you to a place of safety. But she said: 'there is no point, they will only catch up with me again. I shall never feel free; they will never give in'. They took her home and made almost a prisoner of her for three months and even now she is not free to contact us. She is not allowed to use the phone and to come and see us. Family blames us for interfering.

There are some further useful observations made by a secondary science teacher (male, second-generation):

> With the Asian parents, girls' further education can be a problem. My sister and nieces are all educated, so it depends on the family. Teachers ought to help and guide; I certainly do. Times are changing. Asian parents — I mean most — are not willing to send their daughters away from home for education. I think it is a question of educating the parents. We have a home-school liaison teacher. She ought to do it.

All Asian teachers felt that they are trying to help ease the pain which ensues from the clash of values. A senior secondary teacher (female, second-generation) ruminated:

> If they start complaining, I say look I have grown in this environment, I had to fight battles. You must respect parents' wishes. We had some girls (mostly Muslims) — they seem to struggle the most — only one Sikh girl who had problems...for example, this boy used to go out with a Muslim girl. The brother of this girl was waiting outside the school.

> I said: 'you are lucky to be alive, in another situation you would have been dead'. He was expecting sympathy from the white teachers.

A woman science teacher (female, second-generation) made similar comments:

> They have not approached me so far. But I hear from other teachers that girls feel restricted; anger builds up. Yes, I am trying to help. Parents have trust in school. They know the teachers here. He (headmaster) is well liked by parents. It is a very good school. Parents feel OK. They think: 'if you send your daughter here, she won't get hassled'.

I interviewed an experienced social worker (see Ghuman, 1993: 86) who had dealt with several run-away Asian girls:

> ...They have disowned her. She has no chance of arranged marriage. She said to me: 'I am a Muslim girl born in England. I want to do what my friends do: go out and enjoy myself'. Of course her parents were horrified. She would say: 'This is my life, I want to live it my way'. She left home...the risk is that white girls have skills to survive, but not Asians. It took her to the street. A lot of Asian people would exploit her; become pimps to such unfortunate girls.

The system of arranged marriages causes a lot of problems for young Asian girls. The boys tend to enjoy all the male privileges which are part and parcel of the Asian family and traditions. Therefore boys are far less resentful of the situation.

All the Afro-Caribbean and the white teachers mentioned problems relating to the arranged marriage custom. An Afro-Caribbean secondary teacher (male, first-generation) told me a long story:

> This beautiful Asian girl was very unhappy. From school she would go home and stay in her room till next morning. One day I was walking past her house and she came out to say hello. Her parents didn't believe that I was her teacher... They used to beat her up and lock her up. All this because she wouldn't accept an arranged marriage... Some Pakistani parents are very strict: no PE, not allowed to wear jeans or shorts. It was OK in Pakistan but in England it is hard for kids to behave like that.

An Afro-Caribbean social worker, interviewed for another research project by the writer (Ghuman, 1993: 87), was cautious of intervention:

> We must be aware of in-built Euro-centric norms and jump in — we have to be careful of intervention. Girls have to be told of the consequences of their action. They might come to regret it.

Most of the Asian teachers thought that compromise solutions are being worked out by the parents. A secondary science teacher (female, second-generation) explained:

> I am not sure marriages are arranged in the traditional way — they are getting more and more modified. My parents did not know I would be dating the guy I was going to marry. We had a long engagement. I was committed, but I could have changed if I didn't like him. A lot of girls (referring to Hindus and Sikhs) do have boyfriends... Parents are beginning to accept the inevitable. Some turn a blind eye.

A teacher of community languages (male, first-generation) gave the following analysis:

> We are in a third phase now. We got to be realistic. These children are demanding freedom. Parents are changing; boys and girls meet a number of times and then decide whether to marry or not. Then there are parents who are allowing their children to find their own spouses now, because they keep on rejecting — the ones arranged by parents — on trivial reasons. Parents are saying: 'go ahead and do it yourself'. ...Muslims are stricter in marriage, etc. Their marriages are within the family.

Racism and Equality of Opportunity

All Asian teachers, except two, in the study thought that there is a degree of unintentional racism or ethnocentrism in their schools. Some thought it is even overt and intentional. An Asian secondary special education teacher (male, first-generation) put it this way:

> Asian children, in my experience, end up in remedial or bottom streams. They are placed in these streams without any test... A child was put in a low set and told he can't do GCSE examination. His parents came to me worried. I helped that child. He went to a university and did a degree — this is an example of racism. Low expectation of Asian and Black children is common among white teachers. I am very sorry to say that kids in my last school were treated like dirt — they were ridiculed. I can remember children being called thieves, too many in this country, too many having free school dinners, etc. If they could read well; that was considered to be a great feat as if they were monkeys.

A white TESL primary teacher (female, second-generation) also described disturbing incidents:

> One particular woman is a racist; she wouldn't admit it. I suppose a latent one, without realising it. It is definitely unintentional — I think

racism springs from ignorance. What these teachers don't know is that to educate a child they got to know their background and take that on board. To include familiar things in their lessons from their (children's) lives. It is obvious to me — they do it with white kids. Very little seems to make them come alive. It is wonderful when it happens. It is about recognising them as persons in their own right.

An Asian head of a special school (female, first-generation) cautiously endorsed the comments of the above teacher:

Parents say our children should have home-work; you have to hear the white teacher saying why? ...School reports are underhand: they say child is doing well, when it comes to exam options the school says he can't take them. They say his English is OK, but it is his second language. Teachers are willing to accept lower standards from the Asian children. A sort of hidden racism, I think.

A senior secondary teacher (female, second-generation)) responded:

...It is strange that you say that. We were called Pakis. (*Where?*) Not in here but when travelling outside this area. We have Indian citizenship; we haven't suffered. Really, I don't think any of our family has to any extent. It is the way we are: we are fairly tolerant, we shrug our shoulders and carry on. I think it helps. If you start fighting the system, it can get really bad.

Surprisingly, only a few Asian teachers (4/50) met any overt racism. Of those who had, they had to think hard to recollect racist events in their lives. A teacher of modern languages (male, second-generation) described his experiences when he was a student in a grammar school:

I was the only black person in the school, apart from an adopted Afro-Caribbean child. Racism was constantly there — I am talking about the late 70s and the 80s. Oh, sir, he smells; he has got greasy hair; he is different to us; and sometimes physical and verbal abuse. (*What was the reaction of the staff?*) The staff said or did very little. I complained sometimes, and then they would tell them off for bullying. But it was emotionally very distressing; for the staff it was something trivial. They thought I should learn to cope... I remember a French class: pupils were saying his hair smell of coconut oil and the teacher smelt and said it was very nice. That is one way of handling it. But to me, at that time, it was not sufficient. The teachers had no way of understanding a pupil who is Asian and from the working-class background. I never felt I had the support of the staff. Those were very unhappy times. They were the worst time of life, possibly.

A white university lecturer who had an Indian grandfather (male, second-generation) described his school experiences in the 40s:

> I was the only person in my primary school who was non-native. My name is unique — It can easily be mimicked. Secondly, I was quite dark; obviously different from others. My language was perfect. Parents would say: 'Why can't you speak like J...' So I was regarded as the epitome of the upper-middle class as it were. (*Were there any problems?*) It must be said, in fairness, in no sense I was picked on by the teachers. ...It was by the children — peers. Comments and shouts of golly woggy; put my head down the lavatory and the rest of it. It was all very unpleasant and left a deep impression on me. It is a self trap. ...It is easy for others to say — you are over sensitive or touchy about it, but it was particularly nasty. I was in the 'A' stream. Most of the bullying came from the 'C' stream... In the secondary school it was like a magic — the 'C' stream boys left to go to a secondary modern school — I had a wonderful time. My experiences of other establishments have been free from such nastiness: Indeed when I was in teacher training college and happened to be ill, I had the most tremendous support from the college...my feelings (meaning ill feelings) against this country are not rational. They spring from the ground water of bitter resentment of British imperialism. It comes in day in and day out. Inside me I am pleased when England is hammered and smashed to pieces by the West Indians in cricket. It is a silly form of vindictiveness, but it remains with me...having brought up in a culture which tells me the greatness of its institutions: the mother of Parliament; the finest example of justice — the British institutions. This self-regard — unassailable self-regard — this overwhelming arrogance about itself...I find it intolerable.

After fifty years or so the situation has changed only a little as far as the name-calling and racial abuse and bullying of ethnic minority children are concerned. Wright (1993: 32) describes vividly how racial bullying goes on in the classroom. She writes: 'A group of four white boys (aged 3–4) were collaboratively building a tower out of the building blocks. An Asian boy walked over with the thought of participating. Two of the boys were heard to say vehemently, "No, Paki, no, Paki". Another boy pushed the Asian boy aggressively ...Peter...(the) blond headed boy, I noticed that he used to go up to the Asian children in a really threatening way... If the Asian children had anything he would take it off them'.

Likewise Troyna & Hatcher (1992) describe incidents of this nature in their recently published research in the Midlands. There is also extensive case study research published by the Commission for Racial Equality (1989) on this issue. Most multicultural schools now have implemented anti-racist policies, and such initiatives can and do have a beneficial effect in reducing racist name-calling and other racial incidents. As regards mainly all-white schools there is very little initiative on anti-racism. Many headteachers defend the policy of 'doing nothing' to check incidents of racist name-calling on the grounds that it is an attention-seeking behaviour, and it is best to ignore it.

A PE teacher (male, second-generation) told his story:

> I grew up in the inner-city area. I had interest in sport so it got me out of the situation. Through cricket I got out of town a lot. People used to give me lift. I became fairly accomplished in my sport. I went to N... Poly. My achievements are in spite of the education system, rather than due to it. At school they told me I was lucky enough to do 'O' level examinations. (*Was there any form of racism?*) Definitely, there was a covert form of racism in school — perhaps not blatant racism — but definitely a sophisticated form of inequality. ...I went to the same school for supply teaching. I was asked: ' where are you thinking of working?' I said: I want to work here. No, they said, 'go to C ..., that is a very progressive LEA'. I thought they were thinking the best for me, but now I realise it was a fear thing. I knew too much about the school. They (*Who are they?*) senior white teachers are in control. They are happy with the situation. They say: 'it is a multicultural school, promotes equality of opportunity'. It is rhetoric. It perpetuates a sophisticated form of inequality.

This teacher is studying for a higher degree in education and was critically appraising his educational experiences and issues relating to racism. He had clearly thought through his ideas and was very open about his commitments on the ideals of multicultural and anti-racist education.

A primary teacher (female, second-generation) had a different type of experience:

> I met racism in my primary school. The policy of the authority was not to have more than 20% Asians and blacks. So all the children were coached-off to the next town. It was an all-white school. By the time I had reached 4th year there were Skinheads who used to hang around our school. They would do Nazi signs and they thought it was all a big joke. We did not take it seriously. We used to go to the swimming baths and there was a secondary school in the corner. They used to wait for us, and spit at us. We reported it to the head. He had a talk with them. Our teachers were shocked... (*Any racism from your teachers?*) No,

nothing I can remember. Nothing in the secondary school...we had several Asian teachers in the school.

With these few exceptions, the second-generation teachers did not give any specific examples of racism or discrimination. A secondary science teacher (male, second-generation) responded:

I have not encountered any form of discrimination at all so far in my whole life — I don't think I have. People talk about implicit discrimination, they may be right. Maybe I have been lucky at school. There were some teachers who were a bit funny...no, not really, I don't think so.

However, a TESL primary teacher (female, second-generation) recalled an event, by no means an isolated example, of teachers' insensitivities:

During a lesson a child in my class (when I was at school) asked: 'What is a turban, Miss?' She turned around to me and said: 'Your father wears a turban, would you show the class how it is done?' I was so embarrassed because my father is a Gujarati Hindu and not a Sikh. So he doesn't wear a turban... Then there were playground insults and racial taunts for which teachers didn't do anything. In some way teachers expected us to cope with these humiliations.

An Afro-Caribbean secondary teacher (male, first-generation) made a very cynical comment:

Yes, they got racism (white teachers). It applies to Asians as well, but they seem to surmount it because of their own experience of it. Our kids (meaning Asians and blacks) have to work extra hard. We got to be 100% over the whites; parents should instil this in their children. No good comparing it with 'George' who is white...they have to be twice as good.

An Afro-Caribbean teacher (female, first-generation) had some personal experience on the matter of low expectations:

My daughter was advised to do catering. I was surprised because she was a good student. I think a lot of white teachers ill advise black kids...with equivalent qualifications, they (blacks) still have to work hard. It all boils down to prejudice.

A white secondary head (female, first-generation) had some very perceptive comments to make:

Some teachers should examine their own racist attitudes. They would be horrified to admit that remarks such as 'don't behave like a monkey' or 'eat a banana' can give offence. Teachers should be careful what they say and never manhandle children. Also their expressions and emotional reactions to ethnic food, dress, etc. should not offend... Some of the games illustrating racism are quite good.

An Asian head of an infant school (female, second-generation) tried to be positive about the situation:

To me the only way to combat racism and unemployment is to have good education. If they haven't got that they would form gangs and may get sucked into drugs and the like.

There were several positive comments on the situation. A primary teacher (male, first-generation) argued:

I don't think there is any prejudice at junior level, and some teachers really love our children. I try to explain to them customs and practices of the Pakistani community; swimming is one example. Some teachers criticise parents. But if we want to educate children, we must win co-operation of the parents. Sometimes there are problems. A Muslim priest explained to me that he does not want his daughter to go for mixed swimming, but the headmaster was obstinate and insisted that he had the right to force the policy of the school on all children. I suggested a compromise solution.

A white history teacher (male, second-generation) narrated how teachers are trying hard to enhance the equality of opportunity in his school:

Teachers are very understanding at our school. They work to the needs of children. We have introduced Islam in our history course. Religious education is comparative, and two ethnic languages are taught. We invite Imam to take prayers in the school. Our parents governors are Muslims and have a real say in the way school is run...I am not sure about the equality of opportunity in jobs, but here they have it all right.

Separate Schools

The issue of separate schools within the state sector is a contentious one. The opinions of educationalists and parents are divided because of the deeper concerns over the integration or alienation of ethnic minorities from the mainstream, and the broader question of natural justice and equality before the law. The government has recently rejected a request for a voluntary-aided Muslim Primary school. This has provoked further controversy. *Islamia*, (National Muslim Education Newsletter, November, 1993: 1–6) in an editorial, argues: 'This is the grossest of injustices. ...The Muslim community in this country, the mother of democracy, deserves to be treated on equal terms with other religious communities. The failure to grant a single Muslim school grant-aided status will add to the community's sense of alienation and isolation… This decision is a clear example of discrimination against one faith group while other faiths have their denominational schools.'

Asian teachers' opinions were also divided on the issue; but the majority (40/50) thought that, though all ethnic minorities should enjoy the same rights, they disapprove of such schools. There was no difference of opinion between the two generations. A lecturer in Education (male, first-generation) summed up the anxieties of most teachers:

> My own view is that they will become ghetto schools and this would have a negative effect; and we haven't got a Black university…and it is against integration. We should stay within the mainstream and demand our just rights, like single-sex schools… Adolescence is a vulnerable period and needs special care, but it doesn't mean we need separate schools.

A primary teacher (female, second-generation) gave a very functional response:

> I support a multicultural mix within a school. Our aim is to get a job in life. We need to become experts in English. So we need to be in a school where curriculum is delivered in English. Also the gap would widen again between us and the white people. The danger is if there were separate syllabuses… Children will have no experience of theatre — which our children get — is important. Again they will miss out on that. If they are in a Muslim school, they will not share those experiences.

Those who supported the establishment of separate schools argued that they may serve the special needs of minority ethnic communities. Furthermore, ethnic schools may be good in fostering positive self-concept and in realising the full potential of children.

A senior science teacher (male, second-generation) argued:

> …Again, I don't mind that. I am fairly liberal. They have something to offer, like the Roman Catholic schools. Faith is given greater prominence. In a Sikh school kids can learn *Gurbani* and *Shabad-keertan* from the holy book. This can enhance their self-image.

A modern languages teacher (male, second-generation) was all in favour:

> Yes, this could be a possible solution for black children's education in this country. It could be dangerous path to follow — segregation of any sort, but if the system is failing, radical solutions have to be found… It is staggering the number of Afro-Caribbean children who under-achieve and are unemployed, few are going into higher education. Something is going on. Asians are different. That difference may not be

there in 20 years time. Asian family is still strong, whereas the Afro-Caribbean have followed the Western pattern — say goodbye to children at 16.

A PE teacher (male, second-generation) argued:

> Separate schooling can teach kids to be good Sikhs or Muslims or Christians rather than just tolerance of others. I think it is excellent: it can give you your basic identity. The English have a very strong identity; our people can also derive strength from their religious identity.

It is interesting to note that the clamour for religious schools, especially by Muslim and Sikh communities, is growing in the UK. At the time of writing, the present Government has allowed an independent Sikh school to become a grant-maintained school, thus giving official legitimacy to religion-based schools to become state-aided schools. According to Pyke (Times Educational Supplement, 4 March 1994: 5): 'Leading conservatives are pressing the Government to fund religious schools even if they are in areas with surplus places... The 1993 Education Act, passed last summer, allows groups of "sponsors" to ask for their school to become grant-maintained... From April 1 the government will receive applications from a number of schools, including those for Muslims, Christians, and Sikhs'.

Social Identity and Biculturalism

Social and ethnic identities are an important part of one's self-image. Positive perceptions of one's identity can bestow a great deal of self-confidence and boost morale when motivation is low. Research evidence on the linkages between self-image and academic achievement is equivocal, but few doubt the value of high self-image on the general well-being of an individual (see Ghuman & Makin, 1994).

The views of Asian teachers varied a great deal: some argued that the main identity of Asian children and young people will be rooted in their religion; others emphasised their 'hyphenated identities' as in Canada and the US; and a few said they are British because they were born in this country. There was little difference in the opinions of the first and second generation Asian teachers in the study. A selection of opinions follows. A senior secondary teacher (female, second-generation) commented:

> They are proud of whatever they are — Muslims, Sikhs or Hindus. Bengalis kids are being concerned with being Bangladeshis (*What about religion?*) Yea, I think religion is an important part of their identity.

An Asian head (male, first generation) painted a very complex picture:

This is a difficult one... I think they are going to have identity crisis.
They have a problem. They consider themselves British-Muslims or
British-Sikhs. But when he goes out, would he be considered as British?
I am not sure. Some have Anglicised their names so that when they
apply for jobs they are not rejected outright. What you can't ignore is
that they are in English culture and are part of it... But sometimes we
underestimate how strong inherited culture is. As they grow up, they
mature and will come back to their roots. My children would stay Sikhs;
they pray daily. My kids know more about the religion than I do!

A lecturer in Education (male, first-generation) tried to shed some light on
this vexed issue:

They are confused about their identity. Mass media and most white
teachers emphasise the British way of life. They have no way of
knowing our culture; in the beginning they reject our culture. Parents
are not capable of telling them about their culture, therefore the
community must make an effort. Later on they try to adjust to the
demands of both cultures. Some suffer from conflict and tension... In
schools white teachers are mostly in charge of pastoral care. They can't
do the job adequately because it is a triangular process: parents,
teachers and children should be involved. Trendy teachers genuinely
want to help, but they further the rift and take them away from their
roots.

A maths teacher (male, first-generation) argued:

When they talk of identity...perhaps they are more British than Indian
or Pakistanis. They have to learn two cultures: as home culture is
different from school culture. They are coping very well. Parents worry
a lot, but they (parents) are not doing much about it... When kids grow
up they can mix or decide which way they want to go.

A secondary teacher (male, first-generation) of community languages had
a similar view-point:

It is difficult for children to know their identity. More children should
be told about their culture. They know so little about their own culture,
therefore they are confused. Schools are based on English culture and
behaviour. Our parents haven't got enough time and knowledge to
help. Muslim parents are more particular about this; they are clear and
direct about what they want.

A university lecturer (male, first-generation) held views close to the above
two respondents:

Our parents can't teach about our religion, because the majority are not educated. Here (meaning in Britain) Christian priests are well trained; they are graduates and go to theological colleges. Our priest are ignorant; they are obliged not to have any education — formal I mean. All they need to know is the very basics and show a fanatical zeal. Hindu religion is worse than the Sikh religion; it is full of caste distinctions and is very elitist...same applies to mother-tongue teaching. Qualified teachers are not to be found. There are few fluent bilingual speakers.

A primary teacher (female, second-generation) made a perceptive comment:

There are two different categories: those who feel Indians and those who are losing contact. The first group have been back home and have maintained links to the extended family. I think children who are losing contact would be the real losers. They use home language when it is absolutely necessary.

A TESL primary teacher (female, second-generation), who had faced this problem herself, gave a thoughtful answer:

Children go through the phase when they dislike their own culture — it does happen. Joining of two cultures is very difficult. Rather than total identity crisis, they go through an agonising period. Some will create their own unique identity; others will follow their parents' identity.

A PE teacher (male, second-generation) took the situation of Afro-Caribbeans to highlight the issues:

The black identity is based on the American model, i.e. Afro-centric. Our kids should have Asian identity... The problem is that the middle-class Asians have no insight into working-class Asians: some of them send their kids to public schools. Their attitude is if you work hard you get the rewards. If not, you are going to be a failure... In many cases gate-keepers are Asians.

A primary teacher (female, second-generation) regretted her lack of knowledge about her own culture:

We are afraid we may lose all our identity and culture. It is getting less and less. Over the years it would just be brown colour and nothing else, that is the danger... I lost a lot, I want to learn. I regret now that I didn't learn about my language and culture. When I was young I used to say I want to be Westernised. (*Was there any pressure?*) No, there was no peer pressure. We had a very strict life, so I was rebellious as all teenagers are. But now I wish I had learnt more about this or that.

A white history teacher (male, second-generation) had an interesting comment to make:

> In this school the Muslim boys and girls think they have a Pakistani identity. They don't realise how British they have become. They like fish and chips and beans, watch popular TV programmes and listen to pop music. Boys are very fashion conscious; they wear trainer shoes, the lot. Boys can experiment, girls stay more traditional, as you know.

A white social worker, interviewed for another project relating to the identity issue of young people, had a different angle from the teachers (Ghuman, 1993):

> For second-generation it is very difficult. I think it is about becoming bicultural. They have to learn to cope with two cultures. Maybe they would develop new identity for themselves: keep their language, etc. and learn to handle independence and enjoy choices offered by this country.

An Afro-Caribbean teacher (female, first-generation) made an observation on Rasta culture:

> When in Jamaica I used to laugh at Rastas: Reggae music, Haile Selassie and marijuana. I think it is a defence mechanism — something to keep you happy. This way they don't feel alienated. They find a support group. Parents think they are disgraceful ...They are a nice, gentle and kind people... My mixed race children can't identify with anyone — they go with the Blacks.

A primary TESL teacher (female, second-generation) endorsed this view:

> They are definitely going to have a hard time. But they would develop new identities. They are going to make this bridge between the old and the new. But because they are the fibre of the bridge they would remember some of the things are not going to remain the same, if they have to live in this culture. No culture is static; we have to accept that. We need to realise there are going to be modifications which we have to accept. I don't think everybody is going to become English, and the English are going to be Indians. There is cultural mixing gong on: in food, music and fashion clothes.

There is some evidence to support this teacher's contention. Drury (1991: 388) studied the acculturation attitudes of Sikh girls in Nottingham, England and came to the following conclusion: 'I found that my respondents were neither fully culturally assimilated into white British culture, nor entirely encapsulated within their parental culture ...my study on the whole indicates that my respondents were relatively conversant and comfortable with both socio-cultures and, consequently, were sometimes able to exhibit a contextual culture based on selective and situational decisions'.

Parents' Participation in Education

I thought it was important to ask teachers in the study to give their views on Asian parents' attitudes to schooling and education; and the ways in which they can help ethnic minority parents to understand the system of education in this country.

A teacher of community languages (male, first-generation) made the following observation on parents' attitude to the learning of Punjabi:

> Parents are not really interested. They say they want children to learn their language but don't want to play any role in it. They compare it with English; English is more important than Punjabi. The other thing is children never take Punjabi seriously.

A teacher of English (male, first-generation) was more sanguine about the situation:

> Parents can be on the governing body now. But Asians are not familiar with the system. Headmaster can easily manipulate them. The favourite trick is to divide and rule: Muslims against Hindus and so on — I am trying to go on the governing body of the school.

A home-school teacher (female, first-generation) explained:

> Most parents want good education for their children. But they think it is school's business. I have tried to explain to mothers how they can encourage their children by reading them stories in Urdu, if they can't read them in English. Let them go to school trips, look after their health and take interest in what they do at school.

A university lecturer (male, first-generation) was sceptical about Asian parents' participation:

> ...Yea, I think it is good to have more participation. But it is a non-starter; eighty per cent parents are not educated. Those who are, are interested in making money and not too concerned about education. I know this businessman; he and his wife spend all the time in their shop. It is opened all hours including Sunday. Kids are roaming the streets till late in the evenings; they don't care.

A teacher of design and technology (male, first-generation) was cynical of white teachers' attitudes:

> ...To involve parents is a job for a person at the top. By community they

mean the indigenous people. They want to keep the community white as far as possible or if they do want to involve, they want to involve those Asians who have their kind of views. There is no Asian home-school liaison teacher, no head of the department is from the ethnic background (meaning in his school). The reason why they are not employing our people is simply this: our people will import their own values and this they don't like.

A maths teacher (male, first-generation) was sanguine about the situation at his school:

Parents in our school are very supportive, but they don't know the English system. They don't know what is going on; they are really in the dark. (*Do you help?*) Oh yes, most can't speak English, so I help there. Parents appreciate this. Then I got maths books in Urdu for parents so that they can help their kids with home-work. We used to buy Urdu books from Pakistan but they were not suitable. Now we have books written by teachers in this country... We also have a home-school link teacher, so the situation is improving all the time.

A TESL teacher (male, second-generation), who is actively involved in the Asian community, gave an insider's viewpoint:

Our parents come to school when something sensational happens. They need leadership and organisation. I helped parents to form 'Asian Parents Association'. They came to Asian teachers' conference and learnt what was going on. One parent said: 'You have opened our eyes. We found schools as alienating institutions. Teachers used to say to us, your child is very pleasant; but when it came to examinations we found our children not entered'. ...I am a governor of a girls' school. Senior teachers used to say: 'Asian girls have too many problems at home; too may odds against them; but staff is working hard'. I have worked with the parents to change things, and we have seen an improvement.

A home-school liaison and maths teacher (male, first-generation) gave a very cynical account:

Our community is interested, but they are being manipulated. The one who become governors are usually coconuts — they think like the whites. They are already Anglicised. They are not Asians anymore. They are the worst — real enemies.

An Asian head teacher (female, first-generation) touched upon some of the difficulties:

Difficult to develop partnership with my parents and that has been one of the problems. (*Reasons?*) Parents want an open house; they want immediate attention. As you know there are times when I have urgent business to attend to — sometimes I am teaching. I do my best... The English may not do it. I have asked my staff to visit parents; to invite parents in, cook food on the premises, sit side by side with them. This way the barrier might be broken down.

Another Asian primary head (male, first-generation) was more discerning in his comments:

As you know the community is not homogeneous: there are caste, religious and regional differences. So we have a range of attitudes to education and kids' education. There are parents who are really clued up and then those who don't care very much. You cannot generalise.

A science teacher (female, second-generation) gave a similar response:

Parental involvements varies from family to family and community to community. Also there is a class dimension to it. Quite a lot of Asian middle-class and upper-middle class are sending their children to public schools. (*Reasons?*) Motives are not always correct; snobbery and status play their part...my son is in one. They do tend to get better results, i.e. higher percentages passes, and getting jobs is also good. Discipline is strict and our parents like it. (*Any multicultural dimension?*) There is no multicultural education there, anyway far less than the county schools. There is the chapel, and emphasis on Christianity... Parents believe they can deal with the home culture.

An Asian infant head (female, second-generation) described how she has contributed to the cause of parents' participation:

In my school there are a lot of Muslim kids. Mothers thought that I was a Muslim — anyway, they have started coming now. They pop in for a chat. I think they feel at home with me and can talk about their problems in Punjabi or Urdu. Also their husbands don't mind. This is a big relief to them. The number of Asian kids has gone up since I took over. I think it is a good idea to have more Asian teachers in early years... Some Asian kids have hardly any English.

A senior science teacher (male, second-generation) was quite specific about parents' attitudes:

We find Muslim parents to be difficult about their daughters' education. They tend to disappear around the age of fourteen. Attendance gets irregular because parents keep them at home to train them for housework. Yet the Muslim boys are allowed almost anything... Sikhs take education very seriously. (*Any problems with Sikh girls' education?*) No real difficulties. I think Muslims are the most traditionalists.

A modern languages teacher (male, second-generation) gave a deeply personal perspective:

> My father is illiterate from Punjab. He did not come to visit school because it was a daunting experience. Economic factor also played a part; he worked six days a week with overtime thrown in. Language is another factor. It is a big barrier even with the second-generation. Then there is the inferiority complex which they(second-generation) have acquired in schools. Maybe my children will be more involved. Now-a-days if one or two militants get involved, they are condemned by others. Some parents say let them get on with it.

A TESL primary teacher (female, second-generation) had a completely different angle on the issue:

> I don't know…it is good if people are not badgering you; leave you alone to get on with the job. When more parents get involved it becomes very formal: government type meetings. I think most Asian parents are happy to leave you alone.

A secondary science teacher (female, second-generation) confirmed this view:

> Our parents do not participate in that sense. Only on parents' evenings. They are not involved in fund raising or running fetes. It is still the white middle classes who do it… Some help with homework. But they still like to see children achieve as much as possible.

A modern languages teacher (male, second-generation) was very sceptical:

> I find it across the board, they don't respect education. Even a lot of Asian people don't value education… It is very hard. We set up a parent–teacher association. Only half a dozen parents attend; this is out of 750. What is more popular is the functions: prize giving day and multicultural day… I write in their books where is the homework? But never in 2 years a parent has come up and asked me about it. Maybe there is a class factor? Gujarati community, which I am used to, are very conscious. Punjabis are mostly in factories. This is a very depressed area. Our head (of ethnic minority origin) does a lot to promote co-operation: he goes to the local Church and Gurudwara. He is making the effort. Everyone is welcomed here.

A white head of a multicultural school (male, first-generation) elucidated the matter at some length:

> Most parents in my school would be happy to leave it to the staff. But older generation of leaders within Mosques — very encapsulated and in a narrow Islamic tradition — had a strong influence on the local

Muslim community. Parents of the 60s were persuaded to ask for a *Mullah* to be in the school. Lurking behind this worry lies this unease that their children are being corrupted; and this is not too strong a word. The second-generation who are brought up in a more liberal tradition go away to colleges and don't come back.

This headmaster was obviously concerned with the increasing demands of Muslim parents for special treatment and concessions: such as half a day off for prayer, special arrangements for changing rooms both for boys and girls and the provision of *Halal* meat at lunch time. This school has come a long way, though, to provide a good number of facilities for the Muslim students. These include: the teaching of Urdu and Bengali, modified school uniform for girls, separate arrangements for girls' physical education, and the local *Mullah* comes regularly to take morning assemblies.

A primary teacher (female, first-generation) commented on the fact that there can be too many concessions and provisions made in the name of multicultural education. She argued:

Sometimes I think Muslim parents ask too much. Now some Sikh parents are following their example. It can't be good for the kids who have to live and work in this country. They must learn the English ways to make headway.

Another senior primary teacher (male, first-generation) made a similar point:

Muslim parents are very demanding. Every other day they are in our school with fresh demands: Serve *Halal* meat; take them to the big mosque in London and so on. I have seen the head teacher in tears many times; poor thing... I get on very well with the Muslim parents. But I don't think there is good communication between the school and the Muslim community.

A white head (female, second-generation) of a secondary school gave a glowing account of her own efforts:

...it is superb — but you have to go and ask for it and organise it. They don't have the middle-class initiative. I have engineered it. I have a black minister and an Asian mother as a co-opted member of the governing body.

An Asian teacher did allude to the fact that white heads are very manipulative and are engineering the appointments of those ethnic minority governors who will not 'rock the boat'. There is some evidence to justify that comment.

An Afro-Caribbean teacher (male, first-generation) related his experience:

> I am talking from practical experience; Asian parents are more tuned
> to the system. I do a lot of private tuition and most of my clients are
> Asians...for English tuition. West Indian parents want magic to be
> performed in 2 minutes. Asian have no outside interest; only two
> things, religion and education. West Indians are interested in football
> and TV. They get easily distracted. Asians are very very strict and they
> persist...I have tried to do my bit to encourage West Indians to come;
> it is helping matters.

A woman Afro-Caribbean teacher (first-generation) made a surprising comment:

> I feel Asian parents are really geared to education: they are very keen
> and anxious. You talk to parents they are brilliant and lovely. I really
> get on well with them. White parents got their prejudice, but they are
> all right with me. West Indians are prejudiced against me (*Why?*)
> Maybe because I am a teacher and they are wary of me... I don't know
> why?

Involvement in Community Affairs

The first-generation Asian teachers often provided a leadership role in
many walks of life. Most of them were deeply involved in the religious,
social, political and educational matters of the community. This was largely
owing to the fact that they could communicate in English and were familiar
with the working of the British institutions. During the 60s and 70s, Asian
fathers were in the process of re-uniting their families in the UK, and needed
help to do the necessary paperwork for the Home Office, schools and
hospitals. Also they were establishing places of worship, starting schools
for mother-tongue teaching and buying houses. For all these activities they
sought advice and assistance from their educated fellow peers. The majority
of the first-generation (18/25) had voluntarily done some work for their
community.

A teacher of community languages (male, first-generation) gave a vivid
account:

> Most of the Punjabis had little knowledge of English. Quite a lot
> couldn't even write Punjabi; never mind English. I was called on to help
> with hundreds of jobs: fund raising for a *Gurudwara*, teaching English
> and Punjabi on weekends, form filling, purchase of houses, talking to
> immigration officers. You name it and I have done it. In a way it is

remarkable how they coped without any language. It was sheer tenacity.

A maths teacher (male, first-generation) gave a similar account:

I was called upon for fund raising, translation, form filling and liaison with local authorities' officials. They just couldn't handle it. I know other teachers who didn't get teaching jobs in this country, but they liked helping... These teachers also benefited because a lot of them set up small Indian/Pakistani grocery shops, travelling agencies, ran cinema shows and worked for insurance companies... We were looked upon as natural leaders... It was not always pleasant; there were occasions when I was blamed for things which were not my doings. But I am glad I helped. (*Do you help now?*) No, the new generation is OK now, they can handle those jobs. Also I think I have done enough for the community.

A primary teacher (male, first-generation) who is deeply involved in *Gurudwara* activities commented:

Our people were from the village background. They are hardworking and very tough. They came to this country despite the odds against them. Here they worked in heavy iron and steel factories, doing dirty unskilled jobs, and all this without language. I have given all the help I could. In Gurudwara, form filling, teaching English, dealing with immigration problems and purchase of properties. ...In *Gurudwaras* there is a lot of politics now, especially after the 'Operation Blue Star'. Sikh militants have tried to get hold of Gurudwaras' management. Now I work behind the scenes.

A teacher of English and history (male, first-generation), who is an active member of the Asian Teachers Association, gave his observations:

I have tried to rally support for the teaching of mother-tongues. I have tried to co-ordinate the teaching of Urdu for the community. I applied to the Home Office for support. As a result the demand for the teaching of Urdu has gone up. Our community needs strong leadership and organisation so that its voice can be heard.

A teacher of community languages (male, first-generation) developed the theme of organisation:

I am not a governor of any school. I may try for one. I think we should link up with the Black community in B... But Asian communities are split into sections — Hindus, Muslims and Sikhs. And then there are caste difference, Ramgarhia class, Jat class. Also there are regional and language splits... Makes it difficult to push our just demands in a united way.

A teacher of maths (male, first-generation), who taught Urdu at weekends in a Mosque, told about his involvement:

There are classes in Arabic, the Koranic Arabic. Teaching is by rote method. There must be 60 kids...Muslim kids love to go. Sikh kids go to a community centre to learn Punjabi. I go to teach maths and Urdu and also help run the school.

A teacher of TESL (male, first-generation) has been involved in a variety of ways in the affairs of the local ethnic communities. He is also a very active member of the Labour party. He expatiated:

The Parents' Associations were non-existent, so we started one. Within school I have persuaded the management to introduce multicultural dimension and now anti-racist education. I was a governor of a school whose head was Asian, but was immersed in Anglo-centric culture. She was not prepared to hear anything about multicultural or anti-racist education. Being Asian doesn't follow that you understand the issues... Community leadership is weak; they sit and talk and criticise in Mosques and *Gurudwaras*. Rarely we find somebody with active suggestions to improve the lot of our young people who are increasingly drifting into petty thieving and drugs. I am on the governing body of two schools and organise functions for the Punjabi community.

An Asian head (female, second-generation) was involved in community affairs to help the young Asian girls of the second-generation:

I think young Asian girls are in a terrible situation; they need help. I run this Asian Woman Association. We meet once a month. Young people are encouraged to come along. We have social and religious functions. We cook and invite white people to parties. It all helps to break down the barriers. I am also on the board of local Community Relations Council.

However, as mentioned earlier in the chapter, not all teachers were willing to work for the community. A teacher of design and technology (male, first-generation) gave his observations:

I used to; it is a waste of time. There are people who are there to undermine your efforts. There are people who would not let you, unless or until you join their clique. Then you are all right — join their club. I left Community Relations Council... *Gurudwara* politics is not my line. I don't know a single Gurudwara which runs classes in RE. I know a few which run classes in Punjabi. There are no books on the life history of the Gurus.

The second-generation Asian teachers, with the exception of two, are not keen to take up community leadership. They perceive little need for the type of things which the first-generation did, and are keen to develop their chosen professional careers.

A science teacher (male, second-generation) explained:

No, I don't. I don't think I have much to contribute. My dad (he is a teacher as well) is in the Asian Teachers' Association and is a member of the *Gurudwara* committee. He makes speeches in Punjabi and generally likes community politics.

Another science teacher (female, second-generation) was even hostile to the idea:

Sikhism is a very good religion, if followed properly. I don't like the preaching in Gurudwaras. It is the sex inequality that really gets to me. They sing joys of having a son, what about daughters? Guru Nank (*the founder of Sikhism*) believed in gender equality. I am running away from my culture and community, never mind the leadership... Compared to the Muslims we are enlightened, but a long way to go for equality.

A business studies teacher (female, second-generation) endorsed the above views:

Community work is not possible with my commitments. Anyway, I resent religious leaders; they take advantage of their position. I stay away. Then there are in-fights, financial problems and squabbling. I have first-hand experience of these things.

A PE teacher (male, second-generation) appeared to have a genuine commitment:

I am involved with Parents' Association. I have met the chief education officer to get the issues on the agenda. I want to have an on-going dialogue. I am a governor of two schools. We are taking up positions, but don't know how to exercise it. It will come. White heads know how to use their power through their co-opted governors. These Asians become gatekeepers. Also they use the oldest trick from the imperial book, divide and rule. Muslims against Hindus and Sikhs. They are my people, I want to help them.

A teacher of modern languages (male, second-generation) was also positive about his contribution:

I have a commitment to my community. I want to put back something

— to say thanks. I run a football team for the Asian young people. (*Any activities in the Gurudwara?*) No, I don't participate in religious things. I suppose I am agnostic.

Future of Race Relations

A maths teacher (male, first-generation) expressed his opinion:

Politically it is a racist society. But you can't make sweeping generalisations. There are some very good people in this country. They are fighting for justice and fair play for the minorities. Now there is a rise of neo-fascist parties in the continent. It might have some effect here. Wait and see.

Another maths teacher (male, second-generation) gave a cautious reply:

Racism won't finish overnight — it will continue. It is a real disease. I think indigenous people should be educated to the contributions we have made to the British empire and economy.

A teacher of community languages (male, first-generation) was optimistic:

There is a development, but it is very slow. Ten years ago we were talking about mother-tongue teaching. Now it is being implemented by many schools. There used to be one board providing 'O' levels (GCSE) now there are three boards: London, Northern associate, and the Midland... There is more awareness amongst educators and others about the cultural diversity in Britain.

A white lecturer (male, first-generation) with an Asian grandparent analysed the situation in some detail:

I was optimistic up to 5 to 10 years ago; very optimistic...I have little patience with those who expect changes within 20 years. It seems to be positively absurd (*What?*) ...Ah, you could not expect changes in attitudes in the host culture which was a dominant imperial power. You have to look over a period of time. I did not see a single person of colour, black or Indian, any where except Paul Roboson — hero of my father — in my time (i.e. in 40s and early 50s). The notion of a black teacher would have been absurd. There has been enormous changes until the decline in economy. I think for race relations this has been a disaster. It's nobody's fault. Had it been 10 to 20 years longer, I wonder if deep-rooted, if mindless, gutless remarks — 'these wogs taking our jobs' would have disappeared. This is particularly unfortunate because it is a German phenomenon, French and Spanish phenomenon. As unfortunately Western European economies decline, you have the same nasty degradations of ethnic groups. So we have these *Polax*, the

Yougos and then further down the list we have Turks and then we have the Asians. The same 'pyramidical' structure. I was hopeful, provided people did not expect too much too soon — slow cultural changes.

An Afro-Caribbean retired teacher (male, first-generation) also made similar points:

I am very optimistic. People say things are getting worse. They don't know what they used to be like. When I came to England (1942) people used to stare at me. Those were the days: stop and stare. My wife is white. My kids had a terrible time. My big boys were beaten up. Even the teachers were openly racist. We don't have that now. There is a lot more tolerance now, and one of the things which has contributed to this is education. My children grew up with inferiority complex. Black children don't get that treatment now.

A teacher of community languages (male, first-generation) gave his opinion:

A lot depends on the attitude of politician and others. Kids born in this country can theoretically claim equal rights, but the question of colour will still remain. People are brainwashed and still regard us as second-class citizens. Eventually, hopefully it would disappear — but then I am not sure. Like the caste system in our country, it goes on and on.

A science teacher (male, second-generation) was apprehensive:

I am concerned and worried about what is happening in Europe — Germany, France and even Russia. If things go wrong, I would incline not to stay here. I would try to go back to Pakistan. I don't want any hassle... The Asian have a firm hold in this country; it is unlikely. Asians are making headway slowly. In the city centre they have a lot of businesses.

A teacher of TESL (female, second-generation) gave a positive assessment of the situation:

There are regional variations. In some parts Asian are really doing well in business, also in professional jobs. But equality of opportunity is still a problem... The last thing to remember is that culture isn't static.

A science teacher (female, second-generation) was also optimistic:

...I don't think race relations will get worse. If anything it will get better. People begin to realise we are here to stay. Young teachers are good and are promoting tolerance...I mean one hopes it will never get bad. We may be deluding ourselves.

A PE teacher (male, second-generation) was apprehensive:

> I think with Europe 1993 we are getting into the new era which is going
> to see the rise of racism. It will be a struggle all the way. The system is
> not making things any easier. Just as people in the 50s had problems…
> A lot of things are token gestures. Race relations law of 1976 needs
> strengthening, but nothing is being done.

A teacher of modern languages (male, second-generation) was not happy
with the situation:

> Race relations have been the same as far as I remember. Miners' strike
> woke me up to politics. I started to read widely. If anything the position
> of black people got worse under this government. A lot of people in
> France say to me: 'you haven't got the extreme which we have'. I say it
> is in the mainstream, we don't need one. Immigration has always been
> an issue in elections. Can you change people through laws? I am not
> sure if you can — you are contributing.

A science teacher (female, second-generation) was very positive:

> Must be getting better. It is being tackled in schools. There is language
> teaching (meaning Urdu and Bengali) and other multicultural facili-
> ties… But I feel most people give priority to their own kind when it
> comes to jobs, especially in higher posts. Definitely in industry.

A white senior teacher (female, second-generation) concentrated on school
life:

> In our school we have a number of white boys; very few white girls.
> We need more white and black pupils. We are an all-Muslim school.
> H—— is a Caribbean school, white parents don't want their children
> in these schools. Because they will be in minority. So they don't send
> them there. We need a third of each ethnic group. How do you achieve
> this? Bussing is dreadful.

A white head teacher (male, first-generation)) gave a penetrating analysis
of the Muslim community:

> If the Asian community became dispersed we shall not have schools
> like our own. I would have assumed that Asian wouldn't like to. Many
> Asians living here are not purely out of a desire for convenience — food,
> etc. most of them said that if they had the means they would move to
> the outer suburb. Living in white community didn't trouble them.
> Second-generation are now living in middle-class outer ring of the city
> — still working hard to preserve the Islamic tradition, quietly estab-
> lishing their own mosques. Population is becoming more dispersed.
> That can't be bad for race relations.

A white deputy head (male, first-generation) was ambivalent about the situation:

> In education I don't think it (meaning racism) exists. In my experience I have not found it be so. I am trying, struggling to think of instances where it exists. But certainly like for like everybody get the same opportunity...I know it is there in the Police. They have mistrust of ethnic minorities. West Indians are treated in a far worse way. I understand it is in the 'law' too. I fail to understand that. I would have thought living in a multicultural society should have made a difference... On one end of the scale — roughly 20% — people would say if they want to live in this country they should adopt our life styles. About 20% are tolerant and the middle band go with the flow. The middle class areas are still very resentful. Still there is this feeling: fancy selling this house to them — Irish included. I am talking of 60+ age group. I think the younger generation has accepted the situation. But you must understand the vast majority go to all-white schools and they have no conception of multicultural society. As a matter of fact it is more important for them to have multicultural education than us; we have to live it, there is no choice... As time goes on, I think they (meaning ethnics) would be more readily accepted...I have spent a lot of time in Wales. I know there is a resentment between the Welsh and the English. So you have to put the whole thing in a perspective in a way. I think cultural differences do exist and it is going to take time, if ever, to be absolutely normal. To give you an example of food: we got *chappatis*, that is OK. But stronger-smelling food may be a problem. Think of living next door. It is difficult to hold the smell of the food in inner-city areas. At the end of the day, that is in our training and it is highlighted.

Concluding Remarks

What becomes clear from the comments and analysis is that there is a great diversity of opinions on multicultural issues both within the Asian teachers and between the Asian and white teachers. Therefore, I do not think any general conclusions can be drawn from the perceptions of teachers. Discussion on the emerging issues, however, will be taken up in the final chapter.

4 Promotion and Professional Development

This aspect of research deserves an in-depth analysis because of the wide spread discontent amongst first-generation Asian teachers. There is some objective evidence to support this contention. Ranger (1989: 9) carried out a comprehensive survey in England to discover the career progression of ethnic minority teachers. The main reason for the research, in the words of the author, was: 'The commission has received many individual complaints from ethnic minority teachers, as well as general allegations about discrimination in recruitment and the lack of progress of ethnic minority teachers within the teaching profession'. The findings of the research are wide-ranging; therefore its inferences will be referred to in the analysis and discussion of the present inquiry.

In this chapter, comparison will be made between the first-generation's perceptions and those of the second-generation to tease out whether racial prejudice and ethno-centrism are the two main factors implicated in the promotion and professional development of Asian teachers. The reader will recall that in the first chapter I presented an in-depth analysis and discussion of the educational background of the first-generation Asian teachers. In particular, the two major perceived professional handicaps of the first-generation were discussed at some length. These were: poor competence in English, and unfamiliarity with the British system of education and the British way of life.

All the teachers in the study, Asians, Afro-Caribbeans and whites, had a great deal to say on the issues involved in the promotion and career advancement of Asian teachers. Therefore, I have presented the extracts from the interviews in great detail so that the reader can appreciate for himself/herself the intensity and breadth of teachers' perceptions.

Perceptions of First-Generation

A maths teacher (male, first-generation) ruminated:

After five years I got Scale 2.[1] Then I went on secondment to do Advanced Diploma in Education in 1971. After that I wanted to go to inner-city school; couldn't get a job. So I went back. I stayed another two years and applied for Scale 3... I realised I had no chance of getting it. So I became a home-school liaison teacher — half the time teaching and the other half working with parents. In this school there were 90% Asian pupils without a single Asian teacher. Then I started feeling my presence was not welcomed. They wanted me to play a second fiddle.

Another maths teacher (male, first-generation) had a similar experience:

I was a wages clerk in a foundry and after that I worked in a factory. Then I was a bus-conductor for one and a half year. After that I did the course for Commonwealth teachers in Wolverhampton — a short DES course. Then I taught maths in a small Roman Catholic school for seven years on Scale 1. There was a good attitude; they were all Irish teachers. I moved to a large school. There white teachers' attitudes was negative; they didn't even want to talk to me... I have got Scale 2 now after years of struggle. I feel bitter. Our contributions to this country and its economy and to the World Wars One and Two have been fantastic. My own father was killed in the Second War. That is how I feel strongly about it.

A primary teacher (female, first-generation) narrated her story:

I have MA (Hons.) in chemistry. I got a job in a comprehensive school in 1974. I had a lot of problems. (*Language problem?*) Yes, I speak too fast. I was working with male colleagues. They criticised my accent and my practical work. After a year he (headmaster) extended my probation. It was a tough school — there were difficulties, but most were created by my colleagues... In the second school I settled down well. It was a girls school. I had to leave my teaching — I was pregnant. I did my PGCE training in 1979. I took up teaching again in 1983. I was given remedial classes. My inspector came to see me. He said that children could not understand me because she did not understand herself...I have come to D... to teach Asian kids in a primary school. I got Scale 2. I feel I am helping my community here. (*What about promotion?*) No, I don't expect any. (*Why?*) It is the attitude of white colleagues — they feel so superior.

A teacher of design and technology (male, first-generation) had negative comments about his white colleagues:

I have done 19 years in all; 7 years in first school. I am Scale 2. I have tried within school to become a counsellor for immigrant children. The post was Scale 3, but now scaled down to 2. ...Most heads of the houses feel demeaned when they take their problems to an Asian and he or she resolves them. They feel threatened. Only come to you as a last resort. Most English people have still this idea of the Empire, and they think they are great, even the kids. Example: I was teaching history of English furniture. It starts with the Tudor period: 'No sir, you are wrong'. I asked him to prove it. I said: 'Go to the town library and do literature search, and see if you can find an example of furniture before the Tudor period. Then I will accept your objection'. He made a big fuss about it. He did not find anything. I challenged him the next day, but he could not demonstrate it. There are other examples.

A science teacher, now lecturer, (male, first-generation) also gave instances of children's and white teachers' antagonism:

I was teaching preparation of Oxygen — this girl was very disruptive. In a heated exchange, she challenged me to a spelling test. I had to accept. We gave each other 20 words. Fair play; she let me mark it. It was a good-hearted contest. We both got one wrong. Another example, I went to supervise a student in a local school. This middle-aged teacher came up to me and after a few pleasantries started asking me questions about my qualifications: were they from this country or India? I was not surprised as it has happened before.

A teacher of community languages (male, first-generation) tried to explain the poor promotion of Asian teachers:

No, they are not treated fairly. They deserve to be promoted, but don't get it. In my school no Asian or black teacher is in a senior position. (*Main reason?*) Promotion is difficult for all but for ethnic minority teachers it is extremely difficult. (*Language Problem?*) English should not be the only consideration; however if they are teachers of English, I appreciate it. It is Asian teachers' pronunciation which is different but written English is as good as theirs. The English teachers (meaning white) also make spelling mistakes. I have Scale 3 post now, I don't think I would make further progress. (*Any courses?*) I did four terms course at Coventry for the Commonwealth teachers in 1970, and few years back did taught MEd at Birmingham University and have got PhD from the P… University.

A TESL teacher (male, first-generation) gave an account of his experience:

I started teaching in a junior school in 1966. There were 45 kids in my class. It was a tough situation; I was not prepared for this situation. I was good at Drama. I was told I was not pulling my weight about discipline. The kids were mainly from council houses… I left to teach English and maths to remedial classes in a comprehensive school. I got

Scale 2. I tried to introduce multicultural education but the Head was against it. Some teachers were seducing 5th and 6th year Asian girls; nobody took any notice of it. Discipline was poor in the school; kids smashed windows and there was a lot of absenteeism... I moved to this Centre to take TESL classes. I am still Scale 2. I have applied for home-school liaison posts; but I don't even get interviews. White teachers are being appointed to do these jobs: they don't know home languages of children nor they know much about home cultures of ethnic minority children. But the argument is that the best teachers are being appointed. Most white teachers believe in assimilation — well-intentioned, but narrow in outlook. It may be that I have been involved in Asian Teachers' Association and community politics — but there are others in the same situation: on the bottom rungs of the teaching profession. Teachers of my generation, from Indian or Pakistani backgrounds, had too many odds against them. Of course we have certain weaknesses; that some of us did not have fluency in English nor training. Some are educated badly. But some skills were there. The system used them as childminders; mostly in inner-city schools where there was a shortage of teachers. Here is a job; keep them quiet. Our teachers were given rough kids in rough areas; even police couldn't do much.

One young TESL primary teacher (female, second-generation) who has gained her qualifications from this country, had a similar experience:

I applied for a home-school liaison teacher's job. I was interviewed, but the job went to a white woman. (*Can she speak any of the Indian languages?*) No, she can't speak any of the community languages. Everybody was surprised. In my debriefing the person in charge was so embarrassed, she did not know what to say. To the first-generation teachers they used to say it is your accent, your authoritarian attitudes or your Indian degrees. But it doesn't apply to us. I just wonder?

A lecturer, former primary teacher, (male, first-generation) endorsed this viewpoint:

Our teachers are not being promoted according to their ability, experience and qualifications. Their contribution is not acknowledged. (*Reasons? Language?*) No doubt it is our second language and we haven't got the BBC accent. But our knowledge of the language is as good as the British teachers. (*Social skills?*) They are not clearly defined and it is an excuse used to keep us out of senior positions. Some children even think Asian teachers belonged to an inferior race and are not worthy of their respect. (*Qualifications?*) Most of them have done in-service courses or re-training or higher degrees, so that can't be used as an excuse. They have coped with poorly disciplined classes in difficult circumstances.

A teacher of special needs (male, first-generation), formerly a maths teacher, had a long story to tell:

> I had great difficulty in getting a job. Then I did several in-service courses: a maths conversion course but no promotion. So I opened a shop. I was told I can't do both jobs. (*Why?*) You should know, it is my turban. So I decided to go for teaching of the less able, and children with special needs. …Our teachers are treated as classroom assistants. I know an Asian science teacher; technicians used to tell her off, like a kid. She left and went to primary teaching… I am an 'out-reach' teacher, with special responsibility for ethnic minority children, now on Grade C. This has been after a very hard struggle.

An Asian head teacher (female, first-generation) gave an analysis of the situation:

> There are many points — you know I got headship. But it was a very hard work to get one. I was forward looking, still I had to struggle hard. I went all over England, but no good. When it came to appointments, they didn't like my face. It was a sheer chance that I got this job. There was an Asian on the committee. They had to appoint me…Asians have a chip on their shoulder; they forget they have to work hard to get promotion. We have to be *twice* as good as the whites… You know I did two diplomas and a Mater's degree before I started applying. Also to be frank with you our system of education is different in India and Pakistan. People pass their examination by cramming. So it is important to have a British qualification. Secondly, sometimes it takes 10 years to get promotion; we are selective in our perceptions. Asians have to know the system; it can't be on the plate. On the other side of the coin, the panels should be trained to recognise cultural differences in conversation, sense of humour and body language. It is wrong to judge us by Anglo standards all the time. We are different. We want unity in diversity. Asian people have qualities: they can relate in two languages; they can communicate with parents; they can raise self-concept of ethnic minority children. Sometimes panels think Asian teachers can only teach Asian kids, so to get promotion teachers have moved from science teaching to Punjabi teaching or work as home-school link teachers.

A teacher of English (male, first-generation) had a long story to tell about his promotion:

I started teaching in a Roman Catholic school. I taught remedial and normal classes... I did not do any professional course from this country. The only professional course I did was BEd. in Pakistan and had an MA in English and MA in Persian. I have been on short courses on TESL. I got Scale 1 after four years. I taught for another four years and got Scale 3. Then this school closed down and I was back on Scale 2 for 10 years. That is when the crunch came. I was absolutely disgusted and fed up. I don't even remember how many schools I applied to. I was always short listed but never got there. Perhaps my skin colour never pleased them. I applied for head of English and history; but no luck. Then I did a course in counselling and guidance. I got Scale 3 as a home-school liaison teacher in a primary school where 99% of kids were Asians — about 90% Muslims. (*Any Multicultural initiative?*) Absolutely nothing real, a lot of tokenism. I was the only Asian teacher on the staff.

A university lecturer (male, first-generation) had a sad story to tell:

I have been in the department for over 27 years with over 100 publications in the national and international journals. I have supervised several PhD's. A number of junior staff have been promoted with less than half my publications and experience. You can't get far without the recommendations of the head of the department; sometimes he says it is my teaching, other times it is research money. I put it down to my colour. He thinks I should be grateful for the job I got. I wonder what hope is there for the poor sods who work on the factory floor where there is so much open prejudice... I have been to Race Relations Commission; they want a positive proof to take up the case. It is all hopeless.

This lecturer was promoted to senior lecturer and Reader last year after a great deal of lobbying of Deans of various faculties and after he was awarded the degree of DSc. for his original published research.

Another lecturer had a similar experience (male, first-generation):

I have got an MA and PhD from this country. Altogether I have 34 years experience — 22 years in the university sector. I have published more than my previous head of the department: three books, 41 articles in reputable journals and books, and have a position of responsibility in the department. No promotion. (*Why?*) Publish more in refereed journals; do another book; get research funding: this is what I hear. This is despite the fact that my current head is supporting me fully. It is very demoralising. I know for a fact previous years promoted colleagues are not any more productive. (*Reasons?*) First it was the head: he didn't back me. (*Is it racial prejudice?*) No, not prejudice. I think, clash of personalities. Several years went by and the head didn't recommend me. Now it is very competitive. Perhaps they think I am too old.

A third lecturer interviewed for this research (male, first-generation) gave a similar account:

> I knew I wouldn't get promotion. So my brother and I bought a pharmacist shop. From there we went on to progress and now we have six shops plus flats to let. I now get more income from my share of the business than from my salary. I know few other Asian lecturers and teachers who have dedicated their lives to teaching and research, but can't make any headway. (*Why?*) White man loves us if we are two steps behind him, tolerates us if we are shoulder to shoulder, but goes into a rage if we step ahead. Same is true of the medical profession; for the majority of Indian doctors senior Registrar is the highest point in their career.

His comments on Asian doctors find support in the report published a few years ago by the Commission for Racial Equality (Anwar & Ali, 1987: 72). The authors conclude their report: 'Our Survey shows that one in three of the overseas doctors who were not working in their first choice of speciality had to change because they could not get a job in the speciality they had hoped for. This was true of only 12% of white British trained doctors... Overseas and white British trained doctors agreed that the two least popular specialities were Geriatrics and Psychiatry. The overseas doctors' percentages in these two specialities in England and Wales was higher than those of other doctors. For example, in 1981 almost 84% of Registrars in geriatrics were from overseas, but only 9% of overseas Consultants were in General Surgery, the most popular speciality.'

An Asian primary head (male, first-generation) gave the following detailed analysis:

> I fancied primary teaching. I thought it would be interesting. I have also taught in a secondary school and have been a head of an Adult Education centre... At times we tend to exaggerate the difficulties we face. There is a lot of goodwill as well. Let us talk about the positive things. In Edinburgh I got a job out of 80 applicants. When you talk of racism and prejudice there is a question mark here? This is my personal experience; working hard and taking responsibility does pay. I attended in-service courses and sought advice from the head and Assistant Education Officer. I started applying for deputy headship... The major difficulty is the perceptions of the English of Asian teachers. One of the perceptions is poor English; the other what sort of organisational skills do they have? Will he able to convene meetings

and chair meetings? Their other perception is that Asian people are dictatorial — link it with their political system. There is some truth in that. Look at our organisations? Are they democratic? Are people involved?... There is a lot of in-fighting. They would pull the rug under your feet to bring you down. These attitudes do reflect in an interview situation. They should undergo in-service courses — relevant courses. Relevant to the needs of children. That is the advice they need. But they are unwilling to take it, especially when it comes from an Asian colleague. They want head's job straight away. Discrimination is there, but our people need grooming and going through the right channels. (*Have you been accepted?*) Yes, but it took a very long time. When you are part of the system they accept you. But you got be very very good, very effective and mentally very strong to take the hassle. Patience as well... They are OK on surface. I can give you examples... I think also we should not jump to conclusions, if somebody opposes us and say it is racist. Be very careful about that. There is racism, but we shouldn't shout about it all the time. Think what I/we are going to do about it. I say improve yourself and fight not in an aggressive way but in a subtle way. Don't beat your head against a brick wall. Have the right attitude of mind, otherwise it is personality destroying. I always say we are technically deformed personalities because we have racism on our minds all the time. We are wary how white people are going to comment on us on the road, shops or even here in a school.

This is a somewhat laboured analysis but some very important points emerge from the comment. It seems, for Asians to gain promotion, not only do they have to have wide-ranging academic, social and managerial skills but also strong personality. They should also have strategies to deal with racial prejudice. To gain promotion some first-generation Asian teachers had to change their professional interests; for example, from the teaching of the subject in which they qualified to pastoral-care work or community language teaching.

An Asian infant head (female, second-generation) made an important point to illustrate:

I am under the spotlight all the time. I can't afford to make mistakes. I have to be *twice* as good as any white person. (*Why?*) A white will get away with her mistakes, but I will not be allowed to forget it... It does put an extra strain on you. But that is the price we have to pay for being Asians.

The experience of first-generation Afro-Caribbeans is very much like that of the first-generation Asian teachers. An Afro-Caribbean teacher (male, first-generation, retired), who entered teaching as a mature student, described his experience:

> I started as a Scale 1 teacher and have finished as Scale 1. The attitude is you can't go any further. In a way it is tokenism. But you must remember we have come a long way. I came in 1943. I was initially posted for the war. After the War we had a lot of difficulty finding jobs. I was sent by the Labour Exchange for a job. The boss said: 'why do they keep on sending these people here? I must tell them not to'. ...I was demoralised. Then I did two years accountancy course. This man had the vacancy, but he said I am over-qualified for the job. He wanted me to pray with him as a fellow Christian so I could get a job commensurate with my qualifications! Eventually I got a job in the Post Office as a clerk. There were a lot of blacks and Asians there. I worked there for 25 years. In 1973 I heard there is a need for Black teachers. So I decided to apply... Talk about racism and prejudice you don't know how much the situation has improved. When we came overland to South of England, streets were deserted, curtains were drawn. We saw kids peeking out... A little boy hid behind her mum's skirt and said: 'It speaks' as I was talking to my mate. Those were the days when people stopped and stared. I think things have improved. I know they are not fast enough. I remember people on TV used to talk about Niggers and things like that. When I came to Britain as a colonial my mentality was very different, I accepted these insults... I went to Leicester Square in London to a Lyons tea shop after the war. I was in the army uniform. I was the only black man there. This waitress passed me many times. Then one engineering officer came and saw me standing there while other people were getting served. He said: 'This man has been waiting for a long time. What about serving him? He has fought for our country. He fought the same War as I did'. Very reluctantly the waitress served me. I only wanted a drink.

Another Afro-Caribbean's (female, first-generation) experiences were less painful:

> I went to a do course for teaching as a mature student. It was a very practical course. I was placed in an all-white middle class school. I was really scared; I thought I won't fit in with the teachers... I got job in a school with a large Asian in-take. Kids work hard but are very shy... White teachers are prejudiced. It is built into their culture, they can't get away from it. I feel frightened — the way they look at me — as if they haven't seen a black person before. I feel stranger. I will stay Scale

1 teacher. I know black teachers are not getting any higher status jobs. (*Would you try?*) What's the point? I haven't got a chance.

It is apposite now to record the comments of senior white teachers on the situation. They are the people in the senior management who have dealt with Asian teachers and are running multicultural schools.

A white headmaster (second-generation) made the following comments:

Muslim teachers, like other teachers, came from within a certain pedagogical tradition in which truth was framed and articulated in a ready made package. It was there to be received and absorbed by students without question. In a way Muslim and other Asian teachers choose subject — science and mathematics — in which the body of truth is fairly defined. These narrow cognitive perspectives also define their attitudes to others, i.e. their authoritarian attitudes. They can sound abrupt and short with parents and colleagues. We need parents' co-operation rather than confrontation. Then there are other reasons. They came later than the average into the profession because they have to gain extra qualifications, here, in addition to the one they had. That is another barrier. Then in the outer-ring areas the governor might have been aware of the kind of prejudices that were there (referring to racial prejudice) and whilst they would have felt that Asian could do the job adequately, the parents would have made it difficult. In a situation where there is a tremendous competition, they have not succeeded. It is a very competitive world. One is talking about a very small group, a small percentage. (*Do you think Asian teachers are fairly represented at the senior management level?*) I don't think there would be, proportionally speaking, that much discrepancy.

A white deputy head (male, first-generation) made some more interesting points:

Many of them were not trained in this country and they came qualified from abroad. And obviously the major problem was the question of language, but I think we have gone beyond that. The other major difficulty to bring forth is their cultural differences, e.g. if it is Ramadan we need to know, it is Ramadan. The older generation were concerned that this may be to their disadvantage. Dress is another important — it did not fit in. Public school education in their country of origin is very much authoritarian and teachers believed they should not be questioned. In a sense the management used them in translation, as secretaries and general dogs-body. That is not good enough. ...Because of lack of breadth of experience, the system worked against them in promotion and the like. I know a particular case of a head teacher. Her

husband suffered because his language was not good enough. He felt
he should have the same opportunity , but at classroom level he didn't
perform. I think a lot of them didn't build up the right sort of
experiences for further enhancement. In other ways their qualities and
enthusiasm are well used. (*What about racial prejudice?*) I must confess
I have never seen it in those terms. I couldn't imagine there could be a
problem on that account.

A senior white teacher (female, second-generation) confirmed some of
the points made by the above interviewee:

Style of discipline was difficult — very harsh with little understanding
— perhaps too strong a word to use. Maybe they thought they were
there to teach their subject rather than pastoral input to teaching. They
were in school like ours (meaning multicultural) and acted as role
models. (*What about promotions?*) Well they had language difficulties —
heavily accented English. I think a few got promotion in TESL work.
But I know of some schools where there would be positive discrimination.

To conclude this section, my impressions are that the majority of the
first-generation Asian teachers felt that they have made progress in their
careers in multicultural schools where they have specialised in the teaching
of community languages, pastoral work or have become home-school link
teachers. Most of them believe their progress has been affected by the
degree of racial prejudice present in the school structures including that of
their white colleagues. This is despite their best efforts to improve their
qualifications and to contribute in a generous way to the work of the
schools. Their frustrations and grievances became even more intense when
they were told that this lack of progress is mainly due to their language
difficulties and traditional/authoritarian attitudes to learning and teaching
processes. The Asian heads interviewed for the study, however, saw the
difficulties from both the managerial perspective and from the Asian
teachers' angle. They acknowledged that there is racial prejudice in society
at large and in the teaching profession; and that it is a big handicap. But
they were not fully convinced that the first-generation teachers have
actively tried to acquire the professional skills and to cultivate attitudes
which might have secured them senior posts. The white senior teachers, on
the other hand, gave a radically different interpretation of the promotion
difficulties of the first-generation Asian teachers. They thought that most
were handicapped by the fact that English was their second language and
that their accents put them in a difficult situation with the children. One
head thought that their written English was also not up to the professional

standard. Furthermore, they thought their authoritarian attitudes towards their students and colleagues were another big handicap. They believed that the first-generation Asian teachers have served a useful purpose in providing role models for ethnic minority students and in building links between the school and ethnic communities and in the teaching of community languages. They did not think that racial prejudice has played any part in retarding Asian teachers' career advancement.

The large scale survey by the Commission for Racial Equality (Ranger 1988: 40) shed some light on the issues raised in the above remarks. The report says: 'Despite the fact that ethnic minority and white teachers in our Stage Two sample had similar lengths of service (in the UK generally, and in the schools they were in at the time of interview), and had mostly started in their first, established, UK post on Scale 1, ethnic minority teachers were disproportionately on the lowest scales at the time of survey interview. 76% of ethnic minority teachers were on Scale 1 or 2, compared with 54% of white teachers. At the other end, 7% of ethnic minority teachers were in deputy or head teacher posts, compared with 16% of white teachers.'

It is clear that the first-generation Asian teachers' perceptions are supported by this large scale study. The report also comments on the fact that a higher proportion of ethnic teachers are involved in 'community related' senior posts which are funded under Section 11 of the Local Government Act 1966. As regards racial discrimination, the researchers included the following question in the survey: *Racial discrimination adversely affects the career prospects of ethnic minority teachers generally.* 75% of ethnic minority teachers expressed agreement, compared with 46% of white teachers, and slightly more white disagreed (47%) than agreed. Once again we see the differing perceptions of ethnic minority and white teachers. Perhaps, it is worth quoting the comment made by a teacher of Indian origin: 'Ethnic minority teachers are only given jobs when they can find no better teachers — all promotions go to others while we do all the donkey work and are nowhere today' (Ranger, 1988: 56).

Perceptions of Second-Generation

It is important to discuss the responses of the second-generation Asian teachers in order to unravel and understand the complex cluster of factors which are perceived to be significant in professional advancement. There are a number of important points to remember regarding the second-generation teachers. All of them, except two, had their full schooling in this country, and all of them qualified from the UK Universities, Polytechnics and Higher Institutes of Education. English is their preferred language of communication, though all of them can speak one or two of the Indian sub-continental languages. All of them, save three, are teaching in multicultural schools. The majority of the secondary teachers are teaching science.

A science teacher (male, second-generation) made some important points on promotion:

> My father is in the teaching profession (first-generation). Initially it was his idea. He said: 'See how it goes. If you like it, stay, otherwise go to the industry'. He enjoyed teaching, so he advised me to try. He had difficulties; the main problem was that English is his second language. He had a lot more difficulty in communication...culture as well. I have grown up here and understand how 'they' think; the way they act. I went to an all-white school and there was some racial name calling by the white kids. But not from the staff — maybe lower expectations, I am not sure? I would prefer to work in an Asian school because I feel at ease here. I did my teaching practice in one white school and I did not enjoy it because I found the kids troublesome... You get an odd bit of name calling but it wasn't rife. I have no problem with discipline; no more than any one else. Promotion: I think the first-generation raised the difficulties they had, otherwise nothing would have been done. I think they are probably right — in many cases they have been held back. They were not treated fairly, not many white people like to work under black people. In our case we have to try our best. I will stay in teaching. ...There is one Asian head of the house. He was trained here — went to B... comprehensive school. My promotion; it is hard to say. I don't want to be paranoid.

A teacher of modern languages (male, second-generation) gave his reactions:

> I enjoy teaching. It is great and you get paid for it? If I have a future it is definitely in a multicultural school, if not in an all-black school. My cousin is in Grant Maintained school. He had a lot of difficulties. When he told pupils off; parents came up to complain. It is early days, it is his first year. Management has recognised his positive points. He has a lot to offer. But life is easier in a multicultural school... Racism: very definitely, I meet it every day. Yet you have to be careful. When I walk into the staff room I feel it. Whites are in majority; you feel you have interrupted something. They talk against the head (ethnic minority head). Reasons are different for different people, but it is worrying. ...My parents came in 1958. My father tells me stories about this fair country. He loves it here. He has told us stories of 17 men in a house

and rooms used on shift. Really that generation is durable; basically the shit they used to put up with daily, we don't see it any more. They put up with the abuse — Paki bastards. Now if they abuse they would get twice as much back. We got confidence and strength.

A PE teacher (male, second-generation) painted a complex picture:

At school what I suffered was not racism but a sophisticated form of inequality. I went to the same school for supply teaching...I don't think racism is that blatant, those elements exist. Would these white teachers be fair to Asians? I think not. I would like to teach in a 'separate' school. (*Why?*) I believe I can help young kids with their identity. I will also provide a good role model. (*What about promotion?*) I see my future in multicultural or all-black schools...I very much enjoy teaching.

A senior teacher of business studies (female, second-generation) was very sanguine about the situation:

My first job was in a mainly all-white school. I started there on a temporary contract. After that they agreed to give me a permanent contract. There was one other Sri Lankan head of English — married to a white man, very Western. I had no problems... My father was agreeable to carry on with education and thought teaching is suitable because of holidays. At school I have to re-do my English second time. Still there is a hang-up. It takes a little while to do reports — I got a mental hang-up about English. As a year tutor I have to read other teachers' reports. I put pencil marks and leave it to the other person. It got easier as I have more confidence in myself... There are 3 new Asian teachers. They have no particular problems relating to language... Racial prejudice has not hindered my career. I can't say this for every one: depends on the school and the person; how domineering/ confident you are. I was a temporary year tutor and now I have been asked to carry on. I also run a private business: a nursing home. I don't think I want to go further than this. I have a family and kids to look after.

A secondary science teacher (female, second-generation) gave an example of positive discrimination:

I think positive discrimination is very detrimental. This teacher was a sloppy teacher — 50% attendance record, very little preparation. She went for a home-school job and was positively favoured. It is wrong. Another girl was very much into multicultural education and TESL teaching. She had been to Sudan. She was white but knew more about Punjabi culture — she was not given the job. It created a lot of difficulties in the school... People who came from India, it took them longer to get promotion. Racism also plays its part. I know this person, her husband works for the oil industry. At a dinner party they would say: 'Who is going to sit next door to the wog', behind his back. There is a lot of this amongst the middle classes; probably worse than the working classes. Some of the promotions can be tokenism, though. In certain fields — accountancy, computing and law — there is a hell of racism still. They know how to disguise it. I think the older generation — 45+ — were prejudiced; amongst the younger there is very little of it. I would say our people are more prejudiced than the young white.

This teacher was trying to be objective and balanced in her criticism. For her, racism was not always the main factor in appointments and promotions. She was critical of Asian people's prejudices which are based on caste and religion. In particular, her criticism of the sexist attitudes of Asian people was very strong. She thought sexist attitudes are very much embedded in the family and social structures of Indian and Pakistani communities, and that they should try to do something about it rather than always accusing the white community of racism.

A head of an infant school (female, second-generation) also gave a balanced account:

I started teaching in 1974. I got Scale 2 quite soon and then 3 and 4. I did not apply for many jobs to get promotion. I got this job four years ago. (comparatively young age, around 36) ...I think generally Asian have been discriminated. The first-generation had a bad name. They have to be *twice* as good and prove themselves. White teachers came to inner-city to gain promotion. (*Did they get it?*) Yes, they get it quicker than the Asians, which is a lot to do with colour and discrimination. You got be better, one mistake and they say she is an Asian... At a personal level I don't think I have met any discrimination.

This is a very mixed response indeed. It is not unreasonable to say that personal qualities, such as tenacity and being realistic about one's predicament in a society which does not offer equality of opportunity, are important in gaining promotion.

A senior science teacher (male, second-generation) was extremely confident of his ability to overcome any difficulties:

To a certain extent it was my destiny. It was chance...one can only speak of about what one knows (*Almost Witgeinsteinian?*) As far as I am concerned — whether I am lucky in life apart from one case — I have never failed an interview. I have not faced any direct kind of discrimination or prejudice. I am a senior tutor. I get full co-operation from the staff. My turban is recent — 1985. (*Has it made any difference?*)

No, it hasn't made any difference. I am ready for a fresh challenge; I am ambitious. I would like to work in a situation where I can be a role model and ambassador for my people — even in all-white school. I believe in breaking down the barriers. I am equally equipped to teach in all-white middle class school. It doesn't bother me.

He was one of the most confident of the second-generation teachers I interviewed. His self-assurance was based on his previous success in the system. His career advancement, however, took place only in one multicultural school. It would be very illuminating to follow his career development in the near future.

A probationary science teacher (female, second-generation) was cautiously optimistic:

I feel in teaching you will get a fair chance of promotion. Say head of science, etc. It is all very hard work. In this school there is a chance. In white school, I can't say. I haven't had experience of that so I can't say. ...There is a possibility of prejudice. But I haven't met any (*pause*) ...I have in my first teaching practice — in this all-girls white school. I was not getting any help. I needed support. I failed that one due to lack of help. Staff was not co-operative

Another science teacher (male, second-generation) was also positive about his future:

We had a Pakistani gentleman. He was doing his PGCE. He had a very difficult time. He qualified from there. He had a distinct Pakistani accent. So the kids gave him hard time, and eventually he gave up. Sometimes kids are rude to me, sort of too familiar. But generally it is very good. I understand Urdu, that helps... I would like to progress. I am helping with special needs and low ability groups. This is my second year, I appreciate what their needs are. I like it. I hope to go to special needs. (*Any discrimination?*) I don't know. It is difficult at this stage. I haven't had the experience. Maybe I will. So far, no. I will definitely migrate to Pakistan when I retire. I go there every two years. We know it is a poor country, but we all meet in Pakistan.

A primary teacher (female, second-generation) was very measured in her comments:

I was told that a graded post was coming up — purely personal contact — and I applied. Sometimes one is not sure which way to go. I have worked in the inner-city schools and probably will continue. I suppose I realise I have strengths; that these would not be recognised in an all-white schools. Maybe it would be a token gesture, if I was used. The first-generation teachers — my father is one — found it difficult to mix with white colleagues. They couldn't share their problems. Ironically white colleagues who had support from these people have progressed, whereas they have (Asians) stayed in the same positions...I have not experienced any racial prejudice directly. There are different levels. There has been a lot on the media. It has helped me. Sometimes our strengths are not recognised. This head (meaning previous white head) said to me: 'I wish I had an allowance to give you'. I worked hard just like my white colleagues, but not a thought was given to my progress. When I was leaving she thought about it. I wonder? I don't think Asians put themselves forward. They will carry on doing the work without asking for promotion. They are not assertive; they have no training. My father thought about it (meaning headship), and said it is not worth it any more. The time and effort involved, I suppose. I feel he should have... This is home now. I think I am British, but there is a very strong feeling within me that I am Indian as well. They (meaning white colleagues) respect us if we keep our links with our community, rather than if we say we are all British.

A TESL primary teacher (female, second-generation) had a mixed experience:

I feel older generation has suffered quite a lot. They worked as hard as they could — they have been exploited. But my generation would be more aggressive or assertive; both parties realise this. I think definitely there are going to be difficulties for positions of authority. I think it is going to be harder if you are Asian or black. Everybody accepts those ground rules... Promotion in Asian area (community language, home-school link and multicultural schools), rather than your own subject, I suppose?

This teacher failed to get the home-school liaison job, which was advertised at a higher grade than her current teaching post. The position was filled by a white teacher who, according to this teacher, was unsuitable because of her lack of cultural understanding and her inability to speak any of the community languages. There is no way of checking the details of this case but several first-generation teachers made similar allegations. However, there is also a contrary case discussed in this chapter, where a job was given to an incompetent Asian teacher rather than to a suitable white teacher because of the alleged positive discriminatory policy of the authority.

A modern languages teacher (male, second-generation), who had attended an independent selective grant-maintained white school, gave a detailed analysis of the situation as he saw it:

> (*Would you teach in an all white school?*) I am not sure whether I would feel comfortable in all-white school — I am Asian/black person. How white students would view me? I will be worried about their attitude. But worse than that whether I would be taken seriously by my white colleagues and senior management — probably white. I don't know whether it is a paranoia or reality behind it. I think 'they' want to keep the status quo, minimal problems in all white schools, especially in middle class areas. I think it is great here. I found my fears haven't come true. Afro-Caribbean and Asian children have respect for each other and are willing to work together and be friends which I have not seen outside the school, and did not expect in schools. Also whites are involved in as well. ...I applied for a course in information technology and languages. I had a phone call from the office, 'saying' Mr... you have applied for this course. I wanted to check that this course is for European languages. I said fine. She said: 'Yes, all right'. Then it dawned on me that this woman is expecting that all I could teach was Hindi or Punjabi or just another Asian language. These prejudices were there and even greater when the first-generation started teaching... I have an ethnic minority head who is very keen to see the promotion of ethnic minority teachers. If I were in a white school, I would have to fight harder to get up to a senior post, despite my qualifications. I think some people think it is a paranoia, but I am sure reality of it is out there; maybe to a smaller degree.

This teacher still vividly remembers the hurts and pains which he suffered when he was in an all-white grammar school. The perpetrators were his white peers. His teachers refused to deal with this issue of racism. It appears to me that despite his academic success — upper-second honours degree from an established university and the standard BBC accent — he is still left emotionally scarred. His unwillingness to expose himself to a similar situation is understandable: it is a daunting challenge for him to undertake. He is the only one in the study of the second-generation Asian teachers who has candidly admitted the trauma of his schooling; labelling it as the worst time of his life. How many other teachers, I wonder, have suffered from similar upsets, but are not confident enough to admit and face them. Most white teachers appear to ignore racist name-calling, thinking it is one of the things which children do and grow out of it. These teachers fail to realise that such experiences can be deeply wounding and can leave ethnic minority and other vulnerable children emotionally crippled for life. Troyna & Hatcher (1992) show clearly that this practice of name-calling is widespread in primary schools.

A primary teacher (female, second-generation) gave her views:

> I got my promotion last year — A allowance. The head of science left, and I got an internal appointment. I was interviewed by the governing board, deputy head and the head. I have been teaching only for three years, so it is early days to say how I will get on. My ambition is to go for B allowance in five years. This is what I would like to achieve. I don't mind going to outer-ring areas but I would prefer to stay here, because you got the second language and it helps with the parents. A lot of parents can't speak English; you can get through in Punjabi and Urdu. I would be more useful here... I can't recall any incident of racism from teachers. I was in majority 'Asian school'. It was OK. We had several Asian teachers.

The comments of a maths teacher (male, second-generation) are interesting. He is one of the two second-generation teachers who did not have his full schooling in this country. He switched language codes frequently, i.e. using Punjabi and English in short bursts.

> There is no more respect for the teachers. I don't like teaching any more. In an all-white school I was the head of maths department. I was happy there for sometimes. Parents in the white school really respected me a lot. Then others got jealous, including the technicians and the teachers. Then I had to leave. I have my own business and I shall be happy to go for it. Academic rigour has gone out of teaching. I came here to teach for a term — and this is my third year now. The reason is in maths there is a shortage, so they persuaded me to stay.

I learnt from his colleagues that this teacher wants to leave the profession because of his poor class control and general lack of interest. His own perceptions are entirely negative about students, academic standards and schools. He is the only second-generation teacher who preferred to talk to me in Punjabi, though he switched 'codes' frequently. He is the only teacher who had a pronounced Indian accent and was aware of it. He did talk highly of his first school; its academic standards and supportive attitude of parents. I think he was unwilling to discuss the difficulties he faced in his first school due to personal reasons. But he put it down to jealousy.

A science teacher (male, second-generation) was the only teacher who was patronising to the first-generation teachers:

> I am very pleased they are making headway. But sometimes I feel they take on something beyond their capacity. (*Any example?*) It would be

unfair for me to say any thing; perhaps they had a formal training. It undermines people who have full training. I want to make a success of my profession. This is my second year. I think I have done quite well. You got to work at the system; you have to join in and be noticed. I have not encountered any form of discrimination at all so far in the whole of my life. People talk about implicit discrimination, there might be. Maybe I have been lucky. At school there were some teachers who could be a bit funny. No, I don't think so. I feel I am accepted as a teacher and not Asian as a role model. I wouldn't like it otherwise. (*What about promotion prospects?*) I am a hard working person — I don't think there would be any problems for me.

This young science teacher was extremely confident of his abilities. His sister and niece are also teachers and he feels he can overcome difficulties and make a success of his chosen career.

Thus I had a wide range of opinions on the question of racial prejudice and its bearing on professional advancement. On the one hand, there are some second-generation teachers (7) who are convinced that racial prejudice from their white colleagues and pupils is going to hinder their progress and were thinking of teaching only in multicultural schools. On the other hand, a similar number is confident that they are going to overcome racial prejudice through their professional ability and social skills. The majority (11) are ambivalent on this issue, but they felt that they have something positive to offer to multicultural schools and probably would stay in such schools. But the surprising finding is that none of the second-generation teachers gave an example of direct racial prejudice during their teaching or in their school days from teachers — though a couple of them made a vague reference to it. This is one of the most interesting and encouraging findings of the study. A number thought there might have been some teachers in their school days who might have had low expectations of Asian and Afro-Caribbean children, but they did not say anything definite to suggest that their teachers put this implicit expectation into practice. I appreciate the difficulties which the second-generation Asian teachers faced in pinpointing events which are overtly racist, as a different interpretation or explanation is always to hand when discussing racial incidents. Is it possible that teachers did not recollect anything more specific because of the fear they might have felt as children against construing mishaps in racial terms? Or is this a form of amnesia to forget unpleasant experiences to maintain one's self-worth? Discussion on this and related matters is deferred to the last chapter.

Senior White Teachers' Views on Promotions of Second-Generation

A white head (male, first-generation) gave a detailed analysis of the situation:

> The problem they face is this: Over the last decade teaching has become a very 'mature' profession. People have grown and matured within their own schools. Promotion is within schools. In the open market their chances are curtailed because they are up against very severe competition. And the percentage of teachers going to become head of the departments is very small indeed. I was talking to a maths teacher in the school — who should get promotion. But chances are very slim indeed. (*Do you think racism is involved?*) There is a tendency to put down their difficulties to racism. Yes, there is to a degree; and it is founded in experience. It doesn't apply to teaching, though. When I did my research survey, I interviewed an electrical engineer. I went back twice. I was like a counsellor. He was bitter about his promotion. He had reached his ceiling. I think this is the problem. Heads of departments are seen as middle management. Management style varies from culture to culture. There is no ultimate style in heaven as it were. That does create a barrier. Senior posts are very competitive...as the community of Asian teachers grows within schools, modes of management would change. Then a new cultural approach would be a matter of strength. Whether I should be replaced by an Asian head teacher? In some ways I would personally regard that as a mark of success.

A somewhat long-winded comment; but it does point to the major difficulty facing the second-generation teachers, namely of fighting an implicit stereotyped view that Asians have authoritarian management styles in contrast to the democratic style of the British. Also none of the senior white teachers fully accepted the fact that racial discrimination against Asians and blacks does exist to a certain extent and that it might jeopardise the chances of Asian teachers' promotion. Some cynics may dub their attitude as a 'blame the victim' stance, which is often taken by persons in authority when explaining the poor predicament of weak people in a society. This stereotyping was once again confirmed by a white deputy head (female, first-generation):

> With the first-generation, style of discipline was difficult — I have little experience, only two or three teachers I have come across. Very harsh and I think little understanding — too strong a word — maybe they thought they were there to teach their subject rather than pastoral input

to teaching. This is true of teachers trained on the continent as well…
They were good role models. It is very important that children see they
can be teachers. Second-generation haven't got these problems to the
same extent. Again style is little abrupt — but I don't know what that
is? (*A bit authoritarian perhaps?*) Yes, that is what I mean…I would say,
go on do that, please. They would say go on do that. It is far less obvious
in the second-generation. Most of them have gone through the British
schools and universities. They are first class role models, particularly
the woman teachers. They (meaning women) understand the split
culture far more readily. They can be good Muslims/Sikhs and
continue with their education and do what they want to. It has helped
girls in our school. More and more girls are allowed to go to the sixth
forms. Now we got that going (school is starting its own sixth form),
it's going to be OK. Fathers would be happier…I know in some schools
they (Asian teachers) will be positively discriminated. Multicultural
schools advertise to attract as many as they can. In all-white
schools…they are the schools who do need to attract as well. But an
Asian teacher who goes there have to be a very strong person —
discipline wise. They have to be very good to survive, because of
children's attitudes. Yes, they have to be very competent because of
racism of children. It is all dreadful. It goes a long way.

This senior teacher did touch upon the salient points raised by the Asian
teachers about racial discrimination and negative stereotyping. Firstly,
most second-generation Asian teachers are apprehensive that they are still
being labelled as authoritarian by their white colleagues despite their full
education in British educational institutions and resulting acculturation
into British norms and value systems. Secondly, because they fear
encountering children's racism in all-white schools, the majority chose to
work in multicultural schools. Thirdly, because of these factors, the
majority see their professional development and career enhancement being
in multicultural schools. Lastly, some teachers think that they might be
exploited as role models in multicultural schools or their appointments to
all-white schools may be tokenistic, to the detriment of their full professional development as teachers.

It is interesting to note, however, that a comprehensive study on promotion
of teachers (Hilsum & Start, 1974: 95–122) does not mention managerial
experience or style as an important criterion for career advancement.

A white deputy head (male, second-generation) offered an analysis,
which is somewhat different from other senior white teachers:

I must say they (i.e. second-generation) are excellent and the future is very bright. I don't see any reason why they should be held back at all. They are equally good in the classroom. I can't differentiate them in any sort of way. (*Do you think racism is going to affect their progress?*) If you are going to talk to about race relations — I have to ask myself why so many Asian and West Indians are unemployed? I think something is radically wrong. If you go for an interview for a job and if somebody comes from the same club, part of the country, may be wearing glasses? You relate better. Is there a stigma attached to the difference? It is not done in a straight fashion — nasty way. The psychology of this is, if I have to work with this person I should work with my own kind for a lack of better word. I wonder if there is a spin-off. As times go on, I think they would be more readily acceptable. In general terms, I have no experience of racism in inner-city schools; children accept one another, I think that is part of education.

I think this teacher, unwittingly, made an important point on the issue of promotion of Asian teachers. He is a true liberal in all senses of the word. But he thinks when competition is stiff for senior posts, it is 'natural' for the indigenous white employers to favour their 'own kind'. I have come to understand this situation from the Asian parents' perspective (Ghuman, 1993, 1991). Asian parents with resources, especially the middle classes, are inclined to send their children to private/public schools in order to secure the best advantage in terms of social attitudes, speech, accent, manners, style and qualifications. They are cognizant of the fact that the British employers, like employers in India and Pakistan or elsewhere for that matter, have a preference for their own kind, and that it is in the best interest of their children if they were to acquire manners and speech much prized by the English. Asian parents are realistic in the assessment of this situation as racial prejudice plays an important part in the life chances of their young people (Jones, 1993). This does not mean that they condone racism, but naturally parents are acting in the best interest of their children.

Discussion

It is difficult to summarise the thinking and feelings of respondents on their career prospects and professional development as there is a rich diversity to be found in their comments and analysis. It seems to me that the first-generation teachers in the study had to prove their teaching competence and to legitimise their professional status before their white peers despite their advanced and further qualifications from British Universities and Polytechnics. Most of them found their teaching posts in inner-city multicultural schools. In order to gain promotion, a significant number had to quit teaching their specialist subject/s and move into multicultural posts. The two successful heads were in multicultural schools; one being the head of a multicultural special school. Amongst the reasons given for slow and poor promotion were: firstly, racial prejudice from white colleagues and senior management; secondly, lack of opportunity for professional development; and thirdly, racial prejudice from white children. The Asian heads also agreed that racial prejudice and Anglo-centrism are factors in promotion. But they argued that the first-generation teachers have not pursued with diligence those managerial and professional skills which are deemed necessary for senior posts, and that they have been all too ready to blame racism for most of their difficulties. The white senior teachers analysed the situation in quite a different way. According to them, the major impediment to promotion has been, and is, their poor competence in English, especially spoken English. Also, the white teachers thought that Asian teachers' attitudes to children and colleagues are authoritarian which are not conducive to good management style as perceived by governing bodies and appointment committees. The interesting point is that management experience is hardly considered an important factor in promotion by the researchers in this field (see Hilsum & Start, 1974). None of them thought racial discrimination is a factor, but on further discussion they conceded that Anglo-centrism/Euro-centrism bias might have impeded Asian teachers' promotion. One of the other important points to emerge from the interviews with the senior white teachers was the necessity of employing Asian and other ethnic minority teachers in all-white schools to foster racial understanding and tolerance.

A comprehensive study on promotion and careers in teaching was carried out by Hilsum & Start in 1971 and findings were published by the National Foundation for Educational Research in 1974 (Hilsum & Start, 1974). They found teachers selected ten factors, out of 31 desirable attributes given, which ought to count towards promotion. These were: flexibility in teaching methods, familiarity with new ideas, ability to control pupils, concern for pupil welfare, experience in variety of schools, length of experience, good relations with staff, subject specialism, administrative ability and extra-curricular work. But among the ten most frequently selected by teachers as actually favouring advancement were: length of teaching experience (6th), variety of schools (8th), extra-curricular work (9th) and familiarity with new ideas (10th). The authors (Hilsum & Start, 1974: 293) conclude: 'The survey findings were that length of teaching experience partially favoured promotion, though many long-serving teachers were unpromoted. Variety of schools was helpful in the limited sense that two or three schools favoured promotion, especially for women...subject specialism was an extremely important factor. ...One might conclude, therefore, that a correspondence between "perceived", "desirable", and "actual" factors was moderately well achieved.'

Other interesting points to emerge were that the majority (66%) of promotions at secondary level were internal. At the primary level 75% of the promotions were awarded internally. The authors conclude: 'The evidence supports the impression held by many teachers that many promotion appointments are filled internally at school without an open advertisement' (Hilsum & Start, 1974: 88). Attendance at courses was a factor in promotion in primary and comprehensive schools. Age was also an important factor: being between 35 and 40 years old in secondary schools and between 35 and 50 in primary schools 'appeared to have helped promotion holders'.

A recent Australian study (Maclean, 1992) on promotion patterns found that degree holders were at a distinct advantage in secondary schools. The top nine factors which favoured promotion according to teachers are: length of teaching service; conformity with views of advisors and/or superintendents; administrative ability; willingness to move to other areas; personal and social contacts; good relationship with principal; participation in innovative practices; having expertise in a particular subject/method and being a graduate. However, the researcher found, among other factors, the following characteristics of promoted teachers as compared to the less promoted teachers: 'they had spent a shorter period of time in the various schools; they had worked in a greater number of schools; they were more likely to have undertaken further study; they had a higher career saliency outlook; they were most likely, in the case of secondary teachers, to have specialised in history, the humanities or languages in their degree qualifications; and they were more likely to be employed in the secondary rather than the primary school sector of the education system' (Maclean, 1992: 202). In addition, the researcher found men to gain promotion earlier than women and graduates earlier than non-graduates.

In view of the above research findings, it may be worthwhile to look at the perceptions of Asian and white teachers in the study to tease out some of the salient factors which might have adversely affected the promotion prospects of first-generation Asians. It seems to me that the first factor pertains to their academic qualifications. All the first-generation teachers had their first degree qualification from India and Pakistan. The DES did not recognise the first degree qualifications as being equivalent to a British degree. Only those who had first- or second-class Masters degrees were given British honours degree equivalent status. It seems to be that, in the minds of the employers, the vast majority of the first-generation Asian teachers did not hold an honours degree equivalent. This, then, would have been an important factor when appointments at the level of head of department were made. A closely related factor to the degree qualification is that of subject specialism. Most first-generation teachers failed to specialise in their chosen academic field for a variety of reasons. One such reason suggested by several first-generation teachers was that of covert racial discrimination. Whatever the reasons, lack of specialism must have contributed to their poor promotion prospects. Furthermore, it seems to me that as most appointments are internal to schools or to a local authority (see Hilsum & Start, 1974), the 'grape-vine' factor might have been in operation. Asian teachers, as newcomers to the system, probably failed to get into that inner-circle which exercised an influence on their promotions and career development. This is a highly speculative factor and difficult to pinpoint as Hilsum & Start (1974: 293) argue in their book: 'Quantitative measures of other factors (social contacts, conformity with advisers and good relations with the head) are not available, and subjective assessment in such delicate areas would be both unacceptable and misleading'.

They summarised their findings on non-measurable factors: 'On the whole what evidence existed for social contact as a factor favouring promotion was extremely thin. While most teachers thought social contacts helped, it was almost always somebody else who had those contacts — and this from a random, albeit small (135), sample of interviewed teachers of different grades and schools throughout the country.'

In addition, the first-generation teachers entered the profession comparatively late as they had to undergo re-training or gain further qualifications from this country. In many cases they had to do other jobs before entering teaching in order to become familiar with the language and customs of the host society. As discussed earlier, (Hilsum & Start, 1974), age is an important consideration in promotion.

As regards the career prospects of the second-generation Asian teachers, it is premature to make an evaluation. But the views of this group of teachers are varied: the majority (22/25) have a very positive attitude to their career enhancement, albeit in multicultural schools. Compared to the first-generation, fewer of them see racial discrimination as a major factor which will adversely affect their progression to senior posts. At any rate, most of them think they have social and professional skills to deal with racism should it arise in their teaching career.

Note

1. Scales 2, 3 and 4 were approximately equivalent to the later incentive allowances A, B, C and D which in turn were replaced in August 1993.

5 Recruitment of Ethnic Minority Trainee Teachers

It is a well established fact now that the number of ethnic minority students entering the teaching profession is very low (Searle & Stibbs, 1989). The Commission For Racial Equality in its submission to the Education, Science and Arts Committee of the House of Commons argued that ethnic minority teachers are significantly under-represented in British schools. The chief reason given for this under-representation is the prevalence of racism in schools. The submission (CRE, 1989: 1) states: 'In effect the issue is circular — ethnic minority pupils may experience racial discrimination and harassment at school and often perceive their ethnic minority teachers to be similarly treated. The are reluctant to be teachers themselves so institutions providing teacher education have few such students...'

Fair representation of ethnic minority teachers in schools is considered important for a variety of reasons, the chief one being that they provide good role models for Asian and Afro-Caribbean students. Also they can be an important bridge between home and school in multicultural areas; and some of them might consider the teaching of the community languages, religion and culture of their ethnic communities.

The Community Relations Commission (see DES, 1985: 603) have strongly argued in favour of increasing the employment of ethnic minority teachers. The case was made on the following bases: (a) 'It is desirable for people staffing an educational service to be a natural reflection of the make up of the population'; (b) 'People from ethnic minority groups should have opportunities to become professional workers if they have the desire and the ability to do so'; (c) 'Ethnic minority parents and children who are unable or unwilling to trust "authority" to understand their needs are reassured by the presence of staff from their own ethnic group'.

The Swann report (DES, 1985: 604) affirmed all these reasons and went further and argued: 'Ethnic minority teachers may be 'role models' in all-white schools as well as in multi-racial schools, in the sense in which their presence may serve to counter and overcome any negative stereotypes in the minds of pupils, parents or teachers from the majority community about ethnic minorities and their place in our society.'

Therefore, it was considered important to elicit the views of our respondents on this vital issue of under-recruitment of Asian students to teacher training institutions.

Views of First-Generation

A university lecturer (male, first-generation) gave his views:

> This is not high on the shopping list of Asian parents. They want their sons to be doctors and engineers. This is again a cultural import. School teaching is considered very low professional line. For the first-generation it was an achievement. Now they have higher ambitions.

A maths teacher (male, first-generation) endorsed this view:

> Our youngsters are not going to be teachers. Most Asian teachers are over 50. (*Why?*) Those who go to universities...for them teaching is a poor profession. They say better go for medicine. Also compared to other professions teaching is very poorly paid. I think this is important for our youngsters.

Another maths teacher (male, first-generation) made an interesting point:

> Very few are coming forward. Asian children know our position (meaning Asian teachers). We have no authority. They say what have you accomplished? Next generation may not face discrimination. We have to persuade them.

A teacher of English and history (male, first-generation) elaborated on the theme relating to the poor position of Asian teachers in schools and its effect on younger people:

> Not many are coming forward for teaching. They say: 'How many teachers are in good posts? Not many'. They think in teaching there are little promotion prospects.

A teacher of TESL (male, first-generation) further extended this theme:

> The education system works against Asian kids. Career advisors are dreadful people...always undermining the potential of Asian and black children. Usual comments are: 'you are too ambitious'. The common saying is all they want to be is a doctor. Then there are no senior ethnic minority teachers in schools. Kids don't feel inspired to go for teaching. ...It is a tradition as well. Asian parents think of only three or four professions — medicine, accountancy, engineering and now pharmacy. Teaching is lowly regarded.

White teachers' stereotyping of young Asians does not help the situation. A head of social and environmental studies wrote in *The Times Educational Supplement* (Holmes, 1978: 11): '...the young Asian children are quiet, hard working and obedient. After a while it is noticed that some of them are a little unimaginative, and have difficulty applying the concepts learned as the work gets more advanced. As they get older some of the boys tend to become rather arrogant, and girls subservient. Often the over-ambitious Asian parents want them to be a surgeon and no less, when the unfortunate youngster can achieve little more than the average CSE grade 4.'

A lecturer in education (male, first-generation) made some factual points:

> Very few are coming forward — only two out of 700 for BEd degree and three out of 300 in PGCE in my faculty. In Coventry there are 70 Asian teachers I know, not a single person has sent their children to teacher training. (*Why?*) A lot of them were at Scale 1 for a long time. Also they feel there is discrimination. Then the interview panel may unwittingly reject them.

A teacher of special education (male, first-generation) made some constructive suggestions:

> Schools should be committed to multicultural education with head teachers giving the lead. This way ethnic minority children would feel valued. They would think they have a valuable contribution to make with the teaching of their own subject. Most Asian parents don't understand the school system...they don't encourage even their daughters to go for it. As you know Asian parents believe teaching is a good job for girls because of the school holidays.

An Asian primary head (male, first-generation) made a number of points:

> I think there are a number of issues. One within the Asian community; for example, Muslim generally don't want their daughters to go for higher education. So that curtails a lot. In the Sikh and Hindu communities — people like us — aspire very high. In my case, none of my children want to be a teacher. Because Mum and Dad are teachers. They want to be doctors and lawyers...want to move up, rather than down. Anyway, that is what they think. I don't think salary is the main thing. Then when the children go to school and the difficulties they see in disciplining children. How do you deal with such difficult children? They ask me. This is the major factor. The behaviour has gone down the drain. They (meaning young people) see the job so difficult...if they can go for something else, they do. With the National Curriculum and behaviour problems...teachers have no rights to punish. What rights

schools have? Parents have shouted at me and some swore at me. Children see it and young people see it. They really get put off.

Another Asian head (female, first-generation) made similar points:

Very few are coming through the system. There is a serious problem there. (*Reasons?*) Variety of reasons: discouragement by teachers and poor career counselling. Also Asian parents have high aspirations. You have to work at this problem on several fronts. Parents, I think, would be more willing to send girls to local training colleges if proper approaches are made through community network.

Views of Second-Generation

A primary teacher (female, second-generation) commented upon the parents' attitudes:

A lot to do with parents' expectations; for boys only top professions will do. If a boy says he wants to do Classics: Oh, no. He has to do pharmacy. For Asian parents, jobs should earn good money or don't bother. They know there is some status, but no money. This is one of the reasons. If there is a choice between pharmacy and teaching, then they would chose pharmacy...I chose to teach because I thought it would be interesting. It is involved in doing all sorts of basic things. I don't regret my choice.

A teacher of modern languages (male, second-generation) argued:

At the moment, I am discouraged to tell you the truth. I am not willing to work for the people who make me do things which I find a waste of time. I spent hours filling in tick charts which have no meaning to any one else, not even to any other member of my department except to myself — It is a complete waste of time... There should be more Asian and black teachers, but I don't know how? I am not for positive discrimination but perhaps funding and encouragement. Also give them opportunity. Then there is the problem of employment and career development. In an all-white school — I don't want to be cynical — but for any black person to be appointed it has to be for a very specific reason. He or she has to be truly exceptionally good: first class from Cambridge. I can't imagine a white school taking a black teacher unless they have a specific strategy in mind. (*Why?*) Because problems with parents. The usual complaint: 'I don't want my child to be taught by a black man'.

A primary TESL teacher (female, second-generation) gave the following analysis:

First-generation teachers haven't succeeded. (*Why?*) Blame the victim — they have been blamed for their lack of success. This is one reason that sons and daughters of teachers don't go for it. The other is that prejudice is there in teachers like the rest of society. This probably effects young peoples' outlook. I think multicultural is more important for the whites. But it is very difficult to address this in a practical way. Also a lot of parents don't view teaching being a noble profession; no, to be honest. They think if you spend four year doing a degree and teacher qualification, rewards should be substantially more. There is no solution to this problem.

A primary teacher (female, second-generation) gave a positive response:

My father is a teacher. He encouraged me all the time. I think it appealed to me. With most Asian parents status is important. They compare it with India, I think. I think it was valued before...sort of gone down with too many teachers with poor pay and working conditions. I very much enjoy my teaching.

A head of an infant school (female, second-generation) argued:

Yes, I think it is a good idea, especially in early years, to have Asian teachers. It does help in a lot of ways: good role models, communication with parents; and in the teaching of community languages...I think there are problems. Compared with other professions teaching has a low status. Also they think they won't get promotions, when they hear older Asian teacher talk. Teaching is not getting good publicity. It is a hard profession, a lot of work and little recognition. For Asian to get promotion or recognition you have to be twice as good. One mistake and they say she is an Asian.

A head of business studies (female, second-generation) was quite optimistic:

I came to teaching...something I grew up with. My father was agreeable to carry on with university education and thought teaching is suitable because of holidays. I like the secondary age because you can chat with them. For men teaching is poorly paid. Money side of it is not good. I run a private nursing home. Comparable jobs are earning quite a lot and the status, I should think. In my family, girls are let to become teachers because we can have holidays. For the first-generation it was a step up from bus conducting or rail guards. The second-generation are more ambitious.

A science teacher (female, second-generation) stressed the financial dimension:

Asian people are very ambitious. Teaching is badly paid. Considering we are graduates, rewards are pathetic. People with Mickey Mouse degrees (meaning degrees in humanities from Polys and Higher Institutes) are paid double the rate. This is a monetarist country. Failed 'A' levels in computing are getting fat salaries. So the younger generation say: 'Why go for teaching?'

A PE teacher (male, second-generation) gave a different stance to the problem:

> To recruit young people in to the teaching profession we need separate schools. Separate schools can teach to be a good Sikh or Muslim or Christian. This would give them their basic identity. They would love to come forward to serve their communities. In the LEA schools, teachers are racists. To give you an example, I was at a conference of black teachers. This Asian teacher was initially thrown out by the NUT for his views, but now his ideas are taken on board. He wanted to put issues of Asian and black teachers. They are not considered properly qualified. They (white senior teachers) have more respect for caretakers and cleaners than for Asian and Afro-Caribbean teachers. ...They would justify racism through such analysis as lack of English, poor academic qualifications. I think this is the main reason why Asians don't go for teaching career.

This is a somewhat extreme view of a young teacher from the working-class background who has encountered numerous problems in breaking through the 'low expectation syndrome'.

A science teacher (male, second-generation) described the situation:

> Most of our teachers are in science and mathematics; these are Asian subjects. Parents tend to push kids that way, because they probably have done themselves. ...Money factor, I think — that is why they are happier going to industry. Racism is not involved because a lot go to medicine and there is racism there. Maybe low status; and teacher stress is very high.

A teacher of modern languages (male, second-generation) stressed the decline of the teaching profession:

> In a lot of ways the teaching profession has been debased for the last 13 years or so. It has been devalued. Whereas the high-flying professions are legal and medical. Our parents are ambitious; they expect us to be doctors. Students' experience of racism may be a factor. If, as a pupil, you have suffered it does have an effect... But it could also make them more determined...so maybe not important. We could do with more Asian teachers in Arts subjects. I was teaching the other day, kids knocked at the door and said: 'Is this a Punjabi class?' I

thought about that. I was a little bit disappointed — when a brown face is thought fit only for teaching Punjabi. (*Were they whites?*) No, mixture.

A science teacher (female, second-generation) gave a more personal account:

It is true to say that there are not many woman Asian teachers, only two of us here. I personally feel that Asian girls don't feel it is for them. Even the career teachers don't emphasise it...that you can become a teacher. But once they get a degree they like to go for high-status jobs. Parents don't encourage either. I was working in industry, I wanted to change from industry to teaching. I like it very much. I think I am helping Asian girls in all sorts of way.

A maths teacher (male, second-generation), who wants to leave teaching, painted a very negative picture:

I have been on supply teaching for 7 years. I don't like teaching. (*Why?*) Teaching is mixed with administration. And traditional respect has gone. Children's abilities are not developed. Exam results are not good. There is no promotion. Also education has become political. Teachers are social engineers or bank clerks. Asian parents don't want their young people in this job because of these problems.

Views of Senior White Teachers

A white deputy head (male, first-generation) spelt it out like this:

In our school we have 90% Muslim children. They are orientated to family business and teaching is not a way ahead. The role models are from the business world. In salary jobs, their aspirations are far higher — medical profession, law, etcetera. Priority is for professions with high prestige. It may change in future. For example, more and more Muslim girls are staying for further education. At one time they would all say: 'I want to be a doctor'. Now they are more realistic. We have a girl who wants to be a nursery school teacher.

A white senior teacher (female, first-generation) talked about the poor financial rewards in the profession:

Teachers are not paid properly. It is ridiculous: my daughter was offered £18,000 for her first job. This is the top of the spine for new teachers. This is after a degree and PGCE. What encouragement is there? And now students have to have loans because of low grants. So many parents can't support children at a university. It's disgraceful.

A white head (male, first-generation) analysed the situation as follows:

For the first-generation it was a way out of unskilled jobs, and most of them felt it was acceptable. But it was at the bottom of the scale for acceptability. I think because they feel teachers have a low status... The other factor: teaching has low status and always have had. When I compare my senior colleagues with bank managers, who are roughly doing the same job — in responsibilities, etc., they are underpaid. Asian pupils who have ability are very ambitious. They much prefer people in medical, pharmacy and the high-tech side of things rather than teaching...I did explore (he carried out a small survey with Asian parents) whether Asian teachers would be exposed to abuse, but they were not particularly concerned about that. Muslim parents are coming round to accepting girls going into the teaching profession...I feel the most effective way is for Asian teachers is to act as good role models. Sound career advice for younger people and so on.

A small scale research conducted by a team of academics in Bradford, England (Singh, Brown & Darr, 1988; Singh, 1988) throws light on the fact that teaching is not considered as an attractive profession by Asian young people. They gave a specially devised questionnaire to 65 Asian and 42 white sixth form students. In addition, 16 Asian teachers and a small group of white and Asian parents were interviewed by the researchers. Their conclusions are broadly in agreement with the perceptions of the teachers in the study. They found, firstly, that the Asian young people attached significantly more importance to social status than the whites when considering career selection. Secondly, the most attractive features of the teaching profession for both the groups were holidays, job satisfaction and working hours. Thirdly, the four features considered to be the least attractive by both the groups were: low salary, discipline problems in schools, poor promotion opportunities and lack of respect from pupils. Lastly, the Asian young peoples' perceptions of racism in schools were significantly different from those of their white peers. 60% of the Asians thought the presence of racism in schools is an unattractive feature of the teaching profession as opposed to 29% of the whites. Other salient points which emerged from the above mentioned inquiry, and which are relevant to the present research, are summarised verbatim. It is reported that: 'Science courses appear to be the main preference, particularly of Asian boys. Teacher education courses are considered by only a few, generally girls. In the career preferences of young Asians, the teaching profession does not occupy a prominent position. The experience of racism in schools as described by the practising Asian teachers in the group discussion sample reinforces this perception of the Asian students. Their comments confirm the widely expressed view in the literature that racism in schools is one of the major reasons for the ethnic minority teachers' sense of frustration and bitterness'.

Another small scale research in Bedfordshire county, England (TASC, February 1994: 6) also found racism to be the main reason why the majority of Asian young people questioned do not wish to consider teaching as a career. The other factors mentioned were: low pay; lack of encouragement/incentives; parental pressure; and low status of teachers. Some quotes from the students are apposite: 'Teaching is not highly thought of as a career in Asian families. No real prospects...because we don't see role models. We don't think we'll fit in as teachers. There is also a worry about racism and not being accepted and respected by pupils'.

Attempts are being made by various local authorities (e.g. Birmingham and Bedfordshire) to encourage the recruitment of ethnic minority students to teacher training institutions and the appointment of ethnic minority teachers. However, one local authority's drive to recruit more ethnic minority teachers ended in a bad failure (Brar, 1991: 43). In 1986, Ealing education authority decided on a policy to encourage the recruitment and promotion of teachers from the ethnic minorities. The aim was to recruit one hundred and forty teachers to the county schools. In the event, in the words of the author: 'one thing is clear, that in spite of all the promises and alleged commitments to the ideals of equal opportunities, the authority only managed to recruit three teachers out of 140'.

The researcher is in no doubt about the main reason for failure: the members of the panel were all whites who were not free from the negative stereotyping of blacks and Asians. For instance, one of the panel members was purported to have made the following remarks (Brar, 1991: 44): 'The biggest problems with Asian teachers is the inflection in their voice; the accent, purely down to Peter Sellars, even the Asian pupils laugh at them. Sikh teachers need to re-learn English. ...Their perceptions (implying Afro-Caribbean) differ from ours about success. If you can make money via other means, i.e. criminal ways, rather than education, they do'.

The researcher concludes his report by advocating that, in order to implement equal opportunity programmes, more ethnic minority parents should become members of school Governing Bodies and that such parents should have full and open access to information on their children's education. He also stresses the importance of political will in bringing to fruition the principles of equality.

Concluding Remarks

From the evidence gathered and the literature search, it emerges that there are several reasons why Asian young people are not considering teaching as a career. There are factors within the value structures of Asian communities which discourage the entry into teaching. These include: low status of the teaching profession; inadequate financial rewards; and poor chances of career advancement. Then there are forces which are embedded in the structure of the teaching profession and schools. The often mentioned racial prejudice has a dampening effect on young people considering teaching. On the other hand, racism also permeates the legal and medical professions — the two most popular career choices of Asian young people — and yet they tend to apply for them in large numbers. The other important variable is the poor career advice offered by the schools to Asian youngsters. There is evidence to suggest that some white teachers tend to be cynical , if not actively discouraging, of Asian young peoples' abilities and vocational aspirations. Obviously, such an attitude does not inspire confidence among the young people. Recent poor press reports of teachers, schools and attainment standards could be another reason for the poor recruitment.

6 Conclusions: The Way Forward

This research was planned to record the professional hopes, aspirations, progress and disappointments of teachers from the Indian sub-continent who migrated to Britain during the sixties and seventies. As the main objective of the inquiry was to get to know the real thinking and feelings of the respondents, the approach to the data collection is qualitative rather than quantitative. A small number of Asian teachers of the first-generation (25) was interviewed in-depth to gather their perceptions on a range of professional and personal matters including topics relating to multicultural education. Another group of second-generation teachers (25), who had their schooling and professional qualifications from the UK universities and polytechnics, was included in the study to compare and contrast the perceptions of two generations on such problematic issues as racism in schools, the teaching of community languages, separate schools for ethnic minorities and their own contributions to school life. A small number of white and Afro-Caribbean teachers was also interviewed to give a broader base to the research data.

The question which is often being asked of ethnic communities is: 'Why did they come in such large numbers during the 50s, 60s and 70s?' The first-generation teachers' responses varied on this query, but all said that there was an open invitation in the early 60s — especially after the first Immigration Act of 1962 — to come and teach in Britain. It was advertised even on the bill boards: 'England needs 4,800 teachers'. Some gave economic reasons for leaving their home countries, a few were interested in travel and a small number wanted to gain further qualifications. But most of the respondents in the study, as was the case with most immigrants at that time, intended to come only for a limited period of time. In the words of one teacher:

> I had a kind of idealist notion about England, Europe and America. So I left my lecturing job... I had a sort of five-year plan. I wanted to read for a higher degree and at the same time work and save up. The degree

took seven years to complete and by that time the pull of home became less appealing. So I made another 5-year plan.

This myth of return helped them to face with fortitude a lot of the difficulties of social and personal adjustment.

Most of the interviewees had to work in unskilled and semi-skilled jobs — bus conducting being the most accessible — before they obtained a teaching post. Hero (1992: 119) cites an example of an Indian teacher in London who made 300 applications but did not obtain a single interview. The teachers who were successful in obtaining posts were mostly qualified in maths and/or science. Even then most of them had to undertake a Commonwealth Teachers' Training Course lasting for 15 months which, however, was grant-aided. These courses were designed to improve students' English and reorientate their attitudes to educational ideas and practice so that they could teach in British schools. A primary teacher (male, first-generation) explained:

> To begin with I was apprehensive, because I had a Master degree and 8 years teaching experience. But then I realised that my spoken English was not understood...I had no knowledge of the English system of education. There was an opportunity to mix with experienced white teachers doing academic diploma and higher degrees.

Some first-generation teachers (4/25), however, got teaching posts without any difficulty. There were two main handicaps which the first-generation Asian teachers faced: namely, command of spoken English (accent, inflection, diction, idiom and fluency), and their attitudes to children and to the learning and teaching processes. On the matter of spoken English, there was a further dimension to it — one may call it a humorous/cruel side. Indian accents during the 60s became a comedy-hall joke following the well-known and popular film, 'Millionairess', in which the late Peter Sellars played the role of an eccentric Indian doctor with a very pronounced accent. This lead to the stereotyping of Indian and Pakistani teachers and doctors as speaking with a funny and incomprehensible English. The governing bodies of hospitals and appointment committees of schools became very cautious in selecting Asian personnel. This certainly also played a part in making it difficult for Asian teachers and doctors to deal with the indigenous white people.

As regards their attitudes to children's learning and thinking processes, most of the first-generation teachers held an authoritarian stance as compared to British teachers. I carried out an investigation in 1974 comparing the professional attitudes of Punjabi British trainee teachers with those of the British (see Ghuman, 1975). I concluded my research:

'Punjabi teachers were likely to be even more authoritarian and far less child-centred than the trainee students'. In a recent report on Indian schools, Taylor (1990: 331) comments: 'For the majority of teachers and pupils the textbook and parrot-learning remain the norm, by which many teachers require blind obedience and virtual silence from the children'. Of course, this a very harsh indictment of the system and the situation varies from one sector of the education system to another. Nevertheless, the general picture of schooling in India and Pakistan does follow this pattern. The institutions of higher learning also tend to encourage cramming and dependency on set text-books and teachers' notes. This problem was discussed in detail in Chapter 2. The senior white teachers discussed this aspect of Asian teachers' professional difficulty at some length. They were of the opinion that this certainly is/was considered a handicap in their applications to teaching posts and career development. They thought that the current practice of teaching and learning in Britain was and is based on the principle that learning is an active and participatory process, in which discussion and the arguments of pupils play an important part.

Most of the first-generation teachers either obtained their first teaching posts in multicultural schools, which were generally in the inner-city areas, or later moved to such schools to gain promotion. At the time of interview, all the first-generation Asian teachers were teaching in multicultural schools where Asian and Afro-Caribbean children were in an overwhelming majority. A white headmaster discussed the case of a Punjabi teacher who left his multicultural school to teach in an all-white school. This Asian teacher was of the view that he is a professional teacher and not only a teacher of Asian children and 'wanted to prove it to himself'. To his dismay and horror he had a nightmarish experience: racist graffiti, name-calling — and even attempted physical abuse; and little support from the senior management. He begged the headmaster of his old multicultural school to take him back. This incident supports the perception of the majority of the second-generation Asian teachers who think that, in addition to the usual professional problems, they have also to deal with the overt racism of white students and their parents. A second-generation teacher of modern languages, with a very good degree, independent grammar school background and with a BBC accent, summarised the feelings of most Asian teachers:

> I am not sure whether I would feel comfortable in an all-white school — I am Asian/black person. How white students would view me? I will be worried about their attitude. But worse than that whether I would be taken seriously by my white colleagues and senior manage-

ment... These prejudices were there and even greater when the first-generation started teaching.

However, there are a few second-generation teachers, including the ones already teaching in such schools, who would not mind working in all-white or mainly white schools. There are no statistics available on the number of ethnic minority teachers in British schools or on how many there are in all-white schools. However, my own impression from the Midlands is that ethnic minority teachers, Asians in this case, are mostly to be found in multicultural, or even predominantly ethnic minority, schools. And some are teaching in practically all-Muslim or all-Sikh/Hindu schools.

There is some objective evidence to support this contention. Ranger (1988: 20) writes: 'Only 4% of white teachers taught in schools where there were 76% or more ethnic minority pupils, compared with 25% of ethnic minority teachers. 75% of white teachers taught in schools where 25% or less were ethnic minority pupils, compared with 32% of ethnic minority teachers. Not only were the ethnic minority teachers in our survey more likely to teach in schools where there were high percentages of ethnic minority pupils, but they were also employed in far higher percentages than white teachers in those schools where there were pupils of their own ethnic origins...for example, 85% of teachers of Indian origin worked in schools where there were pupils of the same origin, compared with 65% of the white teachers.'

This concern was expressed by the senior white teachers who are managing multicultulral schools. In the words of a white deputy head:

> You must understand the vast majority go to all-white schools and they have no conception of multicultural education. In the outer-ring schools...as a matter of fact it is more important for them, than us, to have multicultural education and ethnic minority teachers; we have to live it and there is no choice.

The issue of racism came up several times in my discussion with the interviewees. This was mentioned in relation to career development and promotion and when I discussed the educational achievement of Asian students. All the first-generation Asian teachers were convinced that structural racism in schools, and racial prejudice from their white colleagues, have adversely affected their professional development and promotions. The two Asian heads, incidentally both in multicultural schools, also agreed on this point. But they thought that the first-generation teachers should have realised this fact of racial discrimination and should have acquired qualifications and relevant experience to counteract it, rather than complaining and fretting about it. Both the heads have good academic qualifications, sound professional experience and an exceptional amount of energy and faith in their ability. An Asian head put it like this:

> We have to be *twice* as good as the whites... Also to be frank with you, our system of education is different in India and Pakistan. People pass their exams by cramming. So it is important to have a British qualification. Secondly, sometimes it takes 10 years to get promotion; we are selective in our perceptions... On the other side of the coin, the panels should be trained to recognise cultural differences in conversation, sense of humour and body language. It is wrong to judge us by Anglo standards all the time...sometimes 'panels' think Asian teachers can only teach Asian kids, so to get promotion teachers have moved from science teaching to Punjabi teaching or work as home-school link teachers.

The opinions of second-generation Asian teachers were more diverse and varied. There were some (7/25) interviewees who held similar views to that of the first-generation teachers, and were convinced that their future lies in multicultural schools if not in all-ethnic/black schools, though only one gave a very specific example of racial prejudice. A similar number of teachers (7/25) thought that so far in their career and their schooling they had not met any racial prejudice and that they would consider applying for promotion in all-white schools. The majority (11/25) felt that so far they could not think of any example of racial prejudice either at a personal or at a professional level, but were inclined to see their career developing in multicultural schools because of the positive contribution they could make to the life of such schools. They mentioned helping with the teaching of community languages, as well as helping Asian girls in various ways, and acting as a bridge between home and school. The importance of being a role model was also emphasised.

The senior white teachers were reluctant to admit that racism is/was implicated in the employment or promotion of first-generation Asian teachers. Instead they pointed out their difficulty with English, particularly spoken, and their traditional style and outlook on teaching methods. There is some substance to support the white teachers' claim. On the question of promotion of second-generation Asian teachers, who had their full qualifications and experience from Britain, white teachers were more positive. All of them thought that even the present generation has some of the professional attitudes of the first-generation (i.e. authoritarian) but in general spoke very highly of their ability and professionalism. This is a cause for concern as the senior white teachers in the study were stereotyping the young generation without substantial evidence. Furthermore, the management style and experience have been shown to have little effect on promotion, according to a large scale study by the NFER (see Hilsum & Start, 1974).

Two senior white teachers also admitted that in a very competitive situation there is likely to be a sub-conscious bias in favour of those applicants who are more like the members of the interviewing panels. This was put down to being a fact of human nature: 'to prefer to work with those who are more like us'. Regrettably, in the name of human nature, many injustices can be condoned.

Perhaps it is this apprehension of unintentional bias against Asians which is making young Asian teachers seek their professional fulfilment and advancement in multicultural/monoethnic schools. This important aspect of the research findings deserves further exploration.

A marked difference of opinion was also found by Ranger (1988: 54-6) between white and ethnic minority teachers on the question of racial discrimination. He found that 75% of ethnic minority teachers, but only 46% of the whites, agreed with the statement: 'Racial discrimination adversely affects the career prospects of ethnic minority teachers generally'. Only 9% of the ethnic minority teachers ticked DK/NA (Don't know/No answer) while 22% of the white teachers did so. He goes on to write: 'Those teachers who agreed with this statement tended to say that ethnic minority teachers experienced far greater difficulties than white teachers in achieving promotion and were often penalised for having a different accent. Many examples were cited of ethnic minority teachers being rejected for jobs when white applicants with less experience and fewer qualifications were appointed.'

Asian doctors who have qualified from the UK are also experiencing difficulties in obtaining suitable positions. Two Asian doctors carried out a piece of research for the Medical Practitioners' Union and found that: 'Asian doctors with ethnic minority surnames were half as likely as others to be short listed for jobs... Statistics have suggested that ethnic minority applicants are three times less likely than whites to get into medical school and, when qualified, three times less likely to become consultants' (*The Guardian*, 18 March, 1994).

This report confirms an earlier investigation by the Commission for Racial Equality (Anwar & Ali, 1987: 73-5). The researchers found that proportionally fewer ethnic minority doctors were promoted to the senior posts of Consultancy, and were concentrated in the least popular areas of medicine e.g., Geriatrics and Psychiatry. As regards career satisfaction, the white doctors felt that their careers had lived up to their hopes very well compared to the ethnic minority doctors, whether they were trained overseas or had their qualifications within the UK.

On the issue of whether white teachers' prejudice adversely affects the scholastic achievement and general progress of Asian pupils, most of the Asian teachers thought that there is very little overt and open racial discrimination. However, some teachers of both generations thought that there are, perhaps, covert low expectations of Asian and black pupils. However, none of the teachers, save one, could think of a specific personal or 'professional' example to demonstrate the validity of this. A second-generation teacher, who had suffered the most blatant and open racist insults from his white peers during his school years, did not say anything against his teachers on this score — though he mentioned teachers' inability/unwillingness to do anything about racial harassment from fellow students.

There is a paucity of research literature on white teachers' attitudes to racism for understandably valid reasons. But a team of researchers who visited schools to report teachers' attitudes to ethnic minority pupils for the Swann Committee (DES, 1985: 236) commented:'The whole gamut of racial misunderstanding and folk mythology was revealed, racial stereotypes were common and attitudes ranged from the unveiled hostility of a few, through the apathy of many and the condescension of others, to total acceptance and respect by a minority'.

Ranger (1988) also discusses the prevalence of racial discrimination in schools, as perceived by the white and ethnic minority teachers in the study. 81% of ethnic minority and 63% of whites thought that there was racial discrimination. White teachers thought that racial discrimination in schools mainly took the form of abuse between children of different ethnic groups. Also many of them said that some of their colleagues had low expectations of ethnic minority pupils — this form of discrimination was also commented upon by the ethnic minority teachers. According to the researcher, over half the ethnic minority teachers in the study believed they had personally experienced racial discrimination; but many emphasised the subtle nature of racial discrimination and felt they could not give any examples to prove its existence.

A recent case of a law lecturer, who had to put ,ip with eight years of racist abuse and discrimination from students, should make the relevant authorities take note that educational institutions should seriously address the issue of racism within its structures rather than blaming the victims of racial abuse. The college victimised this lecturer by cutting his teaching hours and threatened him with disciplinary action, if he were not to undertake teacher training (*The Guardian*, 8 March, 1994).

The prevalence of racism in schools generally has also been commented upon by the researchers in the Swann Report (DES, 1985: 236):'...the widespread existence of racism, whether unintentional and 'latent', or overt and aggressive, in the schools visited. The extent to which myths and stereotypes of ethnic minority groups are established and reinforced by parental attitudes, by the influence of the media and through institutional practices within the schools, is we believe all too apparent.'

An ethnographic study by Wright (1985) shows the subtle way in which the 'low expectations syndrome' may be put into practice in the case of West Indian students. She concludes: 'This chapter...has presented evidence which indicates that the low achievement of some of their ethnic minority adolescents is linked with the procedures of the schools and that these procedures may be causal or at least powerful determinants of pupil effort, performance and attitude.'

Wright (1993: 39) carried out another piece of ethnographic research to highlight the influence of teachers' behaviour on the educational progress of Asian and Afro-Caribbean primary school pupils. She concludes her report: 'Ostensibly, the Asian pupils (particularly the younger ones) were perceived as a problem to teachers because of their limited cognitive skills, poor English language and poor social skills and their inability to socialise with other pupils in the classroom... Afro-Caribbean pupils by contrast (especially boys) were always among the most criticised and controlled group in the classroom... Just as they did in relation to Asian children, teachers often held generalised images of Afro-Caribbean pupils.'

Tizard *et al.* (1988: 172–84) suspect that low expectations are an important cause of the low achievement in many infant schools they studied. But they found no evidence that teachers had higher expectations of white children than black children. However, they were not able to explain the relatively slow progress of black boys in reading and writing as compared with white boys and girls and black girls. The authors write: 'In contrast, black boys on average had the smallest proportion of contacts with teachers about school work. We observed that they received most disapproval and criticism from the teachers, and they were most often said by the teachers to have behavioural problems... In our interviews with them, the black boys were more likely than the other groups to tell us that they have been punished for being "really naughty", and also told off in the playground' (Tizard *et al.*, 1988: 181).

This observation is very close to the one made by Wright (1993) on the Afro-Caribbean boys.

A large scale study by Mortimore and his colleagues (1989: 168), in junior schools, found no evidence to support the claim of low expectations for the black and Asian pupils. They found that teachers' expectations of such pupils were tied to specific knowledge of previous attainment and performance in the classroom. However, the authors are well aware of the fact that expectations can be transmitted in subtle ways and that teachers may communicate differential expectations through covert, often unintentional, means.

In this context it is interesting to quote an extract from a black teacher's (Gilroy, 1975: 90) autobiographical account of her teaching: 'How can whites ever understand our hopes, our aspirations, our feelings and all the sources of our resentment?' She describes vividly how she had suffered racial insults, humiliations and abuse during her teaching career from white parents and fellow teachers.

One of the other major difficulties which the first-generation teachers faced was the recognition of their degrees by the DES. First degrees (BA, BSc.) from India and Pakistan were not considered equivalent to a degree from the British universities. Only first and second-class MA and MSc. degrees from selected Indian and Pakistani universities earned that status and associated degree allowance. This certainly had a detrimental effect on the promotion of first-generation teachers to head of subject departments. This was probably the main reason why so many changed to work either in the field of multicultural education or special education. Those who specialised in multicultural education taught community languages or became home-school link teachers or had special posts dealing with the educational and personal problems of ethnic minority children (also see Ranger, 1988: 66).

From the literature search (Hilsum & Start, 1974; Lyons, 1981; Maclean, 1992) it seems that there are a number of professional attributes and activities which can enhance the career prospects of teachers. Among these, in secondary schools, according to Lyons (1981: 57), the salient ones are the possession of a good degree, to have realised the career possibilities early on and to have worked out career maps, timetables, strategies and sponsors to achieve it. Also he found 'that a characteristic of top-post teachers is their willingness to move schools to further their careers; ...Courses of further studies in their academic subject or in education had also been a help'.

Hilsum & Start (1974: 293) conclude the results of their research: 'The survey findings were that length of teaching experience partially favoured, though many long-serving teachers were not promoted. Variety of schools was helpful in the limited sense that two or three schools favoured promotion, especially for women...subject specialism was an extremely important factor... One might conclude that a correspondence between "perceived" and "actual" factors was moderately well achieved.'

In view of the above findings, which are discussed in detail in Chapter 4, it may be apposite to discuss pro-active actions which may be taken to help Asian and other ethnic minority teachers to realise their full career potential. Firstly, it is important that local education authorities should take heed of the recommendations of the CRE (1988; Ranger, 1988) and the Swann Report (DES, 1985) in implementing equal opportunity policies including those of anti-racist policies. Secondly, the white teachers in senior management should be made aware of the anxieties and worries of the second-generation ethnic minority teachers that they may encounter the same difficulties in career advancement as the first-generation did. Here, the main obstacle could be the ethno-centrism/Anglo-centrism or indeed racism from their white colleagues. This might go under the guise of finding weaknesses in ethnic minority teachers' attitudes, social skills and competence in English. Thirdly, the related problem of student racism in schools has to be urgently addressed. It is desirable, and indeed imperative, to formulate and implement multicultural and anti-racist policies in all schools, particularly where there are a small number of ethnic minority students. Regrettably, it is still considered unnecessary for all-white schools, or schools with a small number of ethnic minority students, to take any action on this front. A recent research carried out in the Manchester area confirms this assumption (Verma, 1994).

As far as individual ethnic minority teachers are concerned, they could improve their chances of promotion by cultivating those skills and attitudes which have been found to be beneficial. It seems to me the first important thing, for the secondary teacher at any rate, is the possession of a good honours degree. Secondly, it is important for teachers, at an early stage, to be fully aware of the available opportunities for career development, and to formulate a sort of 'mental map and timetables' to realise these. Related to this, then, is the acquisition of necessary professional and academic skills by attending in-service courses and, if possible, to seek sponsorship, which can also have a significant effect. Thirdly, experience in a variety of schools has been found to be an advantage as is the willingness to move beyond one's neighbourhood to have wider access to jobs. Lastly, specialisation in an academic subject or educational activity has also been helpful in securing advancement.

The views of the first and second generations on the teaching of community languages are very close. All the Asian teachers in the study would like to preserve the minority ethnic languages. Several teachers expressed their regret that they are not competent in their home language. A second-generation science teacher opined:

> Language is a way to literature. It is unfortunate we are losing it. I don't think it is intentional. It is a shame. It is terribly unfortunate that I don't feel comfortable with my own language. My son understands Punjabi... The community languages are being recognised alongside the modern languages — they used be taught after school. But they should be built into the curriculum, that's where its place is.

The majority wants the teaching of community languages to be part of the school curriculum, though some teachers envisaged practical difficulties in such a policy. Also some second-generation teachers (4/25) think it should be the responsibility of the communities and parents. A detailed discussion of these and related issues is to be found in Chapter 3. It may be noted here that none of the primary schools, where Asian teachers were working, taught any of the minority languages during the school time. But all had after-school facilities.

The salient points which emerged from the discussion with teachers are that, though the importance of community languages cannot be denied for educational, social and cultural reasons, there are a number of problems. Firstly, the question of shrinking resources, particularly deep cuts in *Section 11* monies, has serious implications for the teaching of English as a second-language and community language teaching (*The Guardian*, Education Section, 15 March, 1994: 2). Secondly, according to Baker (1985), the solidarity of the ethnic minority communities concerned is vital. But the sad fact is that the communities are divided along the religious lines. For instance, Punjabi-speaking Hindus and Muslims want their children to learn Hindi and Urdu respectively and not Punjabi as this is thought to be the language of the Sikhs. Parekh (1993: 98), who was sometimes a member of the Swann Committee, describes the fragmentation of Asian communities and their representatives in a pungent way: 'Their Asian colleagues could not have presented a greater contrast. They were drawn from different Asian sub-communities with conflicting interests and expectations, they had no experience of fighting for a common cause, and they lacked deep root in their communities... They tended to speak and act as isolated individuals and lacked collective presence and power, with the result that the problems of Asian children received inadequate attention...' Furthermore, the middle-class Asian parents are increasingly sending their children to public schools where there is a scant regard for any multicultural matters (see Ghuman, 1993). I was also reminded by the two primary headmasters (one Asian and the other white) in the study that most Asian parents are keen for their children to be high achievers and are not too bothered about mother-tongue teaching. Lastly, there is a serious shortage of second-generation qualified language teachers who could implement even a modest programme of mother-tongue teaching. It appears that eventually ethnic minority communities might have to become responsible for the teaching of their language as has been suggested by an eminent scholar in race and community relations (Rex, 1985).

It is important to acknowledge the contribution of the first-generation Asian teachers, particularly those who did not get teaching jobs in Britain, to the maintenance of community languages. Most of the weekend-schools in Sikh *Gurudwaras*, Hindu temples and Mosques were run by these nominally-paid teachers. They often worked against odds in over-crowded classrooms and without proper facilities for teaching. They prepared their teaching material, such as work-sheets and books, for their students. Such a support will not be forthcoming from the second-generation teachers. I cannot but surmise at the waning prospects of community schools in the future.

All the Asian teachers were of the view that little has changed by way of the content and style of the curriculum, which remains Euro-centric. A white head of a multicultural school put it like this:

> The content of the curriculum has not changed. Our curriculum is the same as in the outer-ring area. But our delivery of it is different. Parents want good level of achievements and leave it to us.

Asian teachers thought that they can make a positive contribution in enriching the curricula of schools in various ways.

Asian teachers' views on the educational progress of Asian students were varied. The majority thought that Asian students' performance ranges from average to the above average. Some felt that the performance of Asian pupils is often compared with that of white children from the lower socio-economic background and theréfore appears better than what it really is. The Asian teachers mentioned a number of factors which affect their progress at school: low expectations of some white teachers; poor command of English and English being the second language of some students; poor quality of teaching; and a lack of home-support in some ethnic communities. A wide-ranging study by Smith & Tomlinson (1989: 305) on the achievement of black and Asian pupils concluded: 'At the point of entry to secondary school, certain categories of South Asian children scored substantially lower in reading and maths than the average for the children tested. The low scoring groups were Moslems originating from Bangladesh and Pakistan, whereas Sikhs and Hindus achieved average or above average scores'.

A more recent report by the Policy Studies Institute (Jones, 1993) supports the findings of the above study. However, a perceptive analysis and comments by Eggleston (1992: 21) on Smith & Tomlinson's (1989) data on the achievement pattern of ethnic minority students should be taken seriously. He writes: '...that in many inner city schools, black children could and should do better than the norm for the often low-aspiring white children who shared their schools. To suggest that the highest level of white attainment in any school must also mark the upper level of achievement for black children is, perhaps, one of the most oppressive forms of racism and racist comment...'

Asian teachers thought that they can make a significant contribution in raising the self-image of Asian children and young people and hopefully this could lead to higher levels of attainment.

Competence of Asian pupils' in English is a cause for concern for both Asian and white teachers in the study. The majority of Asian teachers thought that children who were born in Britain and went to playgroups and nursery schools, are well prepared to learn English at school. However, doubts were expressed regarding the level of interest and ability of some parents in providing active support for their youngsters to learn English. A white teacher, in charge of a TESL unit in a comprehensive school, gave a pessimistic response: '80% of kids need some sort of language support in my school'. There is evidence to suggest that Asian children, particularly of Pakistani and Bangladeshi origins, are achieving poor grades in reading and writing (Tizard et al., 1988; Smith & Tomlinson, 1989). A white teacher illustrated:

> They all communicate well, but there is distinct advantage to black and white children. They can use idioms and have richer vocabulary than Muslim kids. Even if they are not bright, they can use metaphors and idioms with ease. For instance, kids in my class did not know 'thigh'...they have a restricted vocabulary. Even when kids were born here, English is still not their first language. Of course a lot depends on the home background. If a family is English -speaking it is all right.

On the question of separate schools, the opinions of Asian teachers were divided, as is the case within the community and society at large. However, the majority thought that, although personally they don't approve of such schools, the Asian communities should enjoy the same rights and privileges as the other minorities in the UK have had over a long period of time. A first-generation lecturer summed up the feelings of the Asian teachers:

> ...They will become ghetto schools and this will have a negative effect; and we haven't got a black university...and it is against integration. We should stay within the mainstream and demand our just rights, like single-sex schools.

Fears were expressed that separate schools may further disadvantage Asian children, particularly their competence in English, and this might lower their chances of successfully competing for jobs in the open market where racial discrimination is rife. But a few teachers believed that such schools can raise children's self-concept. A second-generation PE teacher was very enthusiastic:

> Separate schools can teach kids to be good Sikhs or Muslims or Christians rather than just tolerance of other religions. I think it is excellent; it can give you your basic identity. The English have a very strong identity — our people can derive strength from their religious identity.

The present government has given permission to a Sikh school to opt in, i.e. to become direct grant-maintained from being a private school — the first ethnic minority school to have done so under the provision of the new Education Act of 1993 (*Times Educational Supplement*, 4 March, 1994: 5). According to the white deputy head of the school: 'Sikh parents choose the school because they fear their children are in danger of losing their religion, culture and identity. The college teaches Punjabi; religious education is based on Sikh studies and children are introduced to classical Sikh religious music'.

The call for separate schools also comes from an experienced black headmaster, Carlton Duncan (1992: 25), who argues 'that institutional racism makes it impossible for the black child (meaning Asian and Afro-Caribbean) to get a fair deal in the British school system'.

Asian teachers' comments on the social identity of young Asian students were varied. The majority argued that their core identity will be based on their respective religions; some thought it will be hyphenated as in Canada and America; and a few, including white teachers, said it would be British because they were born in this country. An Asian head, first-generation, explained:

> I think they are going to have identity crisis. They have a problem. They consider themselves British-Muslim or British-Sikh, but when they go out, would they be considered British? I am not sure. Some have

Anglicised their names so that when they apply for jobs they are not rejected outright.

However, despite wide-ranging comments, the majority of teachers said that most young people are sensibly learning the elements of both cultures and are capable of functioning in both — a sort of developing bicultural identity. Some second-generation teachers expressed regret that they were not given the opportunity to learn more about their history and culture. They were determined that their own children will be given ample facilities to do so.

Their views on parents' participation were also very diverse. The comments of a second-generation Asian teacher sums up the situation:

> Parental involvement varies from family to family and community to community. Also there is a class dimension to it. Quite a lot of Asian middle-class and upper-middle class parents are sending their children to public school — motives are not always correct, snobbery and status play their part... They tend to get better results, i.e. higher percentages passes, and getting job is also good. Discipline is good and our parents like it.

Some Asian teachers thought that even the second-generation find it a daunting experience to go to school on a parents' day. Amongst the factors mentioned were: shift work; their poor English; and an inferiority complex which some of them have acquired at school. It appears that there is still a need for schools to make special efforts to attract Asian and Afro-Caribbean parents to schools. These may include the presence of bilingual teachers, and times and venues of meetings should be so arranged that they are not inconvenient to parents. I was told of the laudable efforts of a black headmaster to involve parents in school activities. He visited the local Sikh *Gurudawara* and Church to drum up support from the ethnic minority parents. This is one area of activity in which the Asian teachers have made and are making a substantial contribution. The senior white teachers were full of praise, particularly for first-generation teachers, for helping with translation work, talking to and reassuring parents on various school policies, and informing white teachers of minority parents' concerns. An Asian female infant head (second-generation) described her contribution:

> In my school there are a lot of Muslim kids. Mothers thought that I was a Muslim...anyway, they have started coming now. They pop in for a chat; I think they feel at home with me and can talk about their problems in Punjabi or Urdu. Also their husbands don't mind. This is a big relief to them. The number of Asian kids have gone up since I took over. I

think it is a good idea to have more Asian teachers in early years — some Asian kids have hardly any English.

The first-generation Asian teachers also contributed generously to the social welfare of their communities. A high proportion of Asian immigrants was from a rural background with little knowledge of English. This involvement meant translation work, leadership roles, help in rebuilding some of the ethnic community institutions such as *Gurudwaras* and Mosques, sorting out immigration problems, liaison with local authority officers and in a variety of other ways.

The second-generation teachers do not participate to the same extent, though some are very committed. This is partly to do with the changing circumstances of the ethnic minorities in this country; for example, young people in the family can help with 'English and translation' which were the two major problems. The second-generation seems to be secular and broad in their outlook and they see their role as being within the wider society, e.g. in local and national politics or trade union activities.

It has been amply demonstrated (see Chapter 5) that there is a real problem in attracting young Asians to the teaching profession. The reasons for this situation lie both within the value systems and attitudes of the Asian communities and within the organisation and structure of the schools and the teaching profession. In India and Pakistan, the status of teachers is very low and their pay is poor. The majority of teachers work in private schools where they are not even paid a minimum statuary salary, and the working conditions can be quite bad. A significant number of Asian teachers emigrated to the UK for this very reason. Asian parents' poor perceptions of the teaching profession are coloured by this experience. Most young people of Asian origin have met some form of overt or covert racism in schools — it may not be necessarily from the teachers, but from their white peers. Also, probably, they have come across very many Asian teachers who have had a difficult time at school. The first-generation teachers, particularly, had to put up with racial abuse and challenges to their authority from some white pupils and maybe from some white colleagues. Then there are many anecdotal stories of Asian teachers who didn't get promotion despite their rich experience, good qualifications and substantial contribution to the life of schools. Whether these stories are authentic or not does not seem to matter, for the perceptions of most Asian young people are based on such evidence, according to the Asian teachers in the study. A study by Singh (1988) discusses the views of Asian young people for not choosing teaching as a career. Amongst the various factors mentioned, racism in schools is given as one of the reasons, as are the negative perceptions of the Asian community to teaching. Then there are concerns about teaching which they share with their white peers. These include: low salaries, discipline problems, the pressures of the National Curriculum, and large classes.

Some researchers (Blair, 1992; Siraj-Blatchford, 1991) have underlined factors within the teacher training institutions which need addressing. The first one relates to the 'low expectations' of ethnic minority trainee teachers, as far as their use of English is concerned. According to these authors, this is often a stereotyped picture rather than a reality. A second problem relates to the fact that ethnic teachers often encounter racism from white pupils and there is little support forthcoming from the school staff (where they do their teaching practice) and from their tutors. One second-generation teacher in the study related how she encountered such a situation:

> I have met prejudice in my first teaching practice. In this all-white girls school, I was not getting any help. I needed support, I failed that one due to lack of help. Staff was not co-operative.

Another second-generation woman teacher thought that grading given to ethnic minority teachers seemed to be somewhat lower, but she was rather vague about it. The Commission for Racial Equality (1989: 3), in its submission to the House of Commons, also expressed concern over students' predicament in training institutions: 'We have been told by ethnic minority student teachers that they often feel isolated, stereotyped by other students and perceived as 'representative' of their communities, thus inhibiting them in all aspects of their study and leisure activities'.

An investigation by Siraj-Blatchford (1991: 43) found that a significant majority of black student teachers had to face racism during their teaching practice, both from their fellow students and lecturers and in the content of courses. The researchers have quoted students' comments in the report to illustrate the nature of racist incidents. Two are worth repeating: (1) 'A lecturer was downgrading their work and victimising them because they had challenged him on race and equal opportunities issues'. (2) 'I went for an interview in a school where about 10% of the pupils were from ethnic minorities. I didn't get the position, but the principal kindly informed me that the reference he had from the School of Education lecturer (my science group tutor) over the telephone had said: "She will be most suitable to a school like..." which is a mainly multi-ethnic school'.

None of the second-generation Asian teachers, save one, gave such a grave account of their training experience. This teacher said that much antipathy — almost active hostility — developed between a group of fellow students and two lecturers in multicultural education. This situation came about because one of the lecturers concerned made a very cutting and derogatory remark about the teaching of Shakespeare's dramas to children in schools.

A recent committee of inquiry into the high failure rate of ethnic minority students (three times the whites) at a Bar Law school found no evidence of alleged direct or indirect racial discrimination. But it attributed the minority's poor examination results to the failure of the institutions to meet their needs. The report's recommendations include: 'an overhaul of the assessment system and external examinations and double marking. There appeared to have been tutors' bias in marking and general assessment' (*The Guardian*, 13 April, 1994: 3). A report commissioned by the Law society found strong evidence to support the fact that ethnic minority students are discriminated against by solicitors when applying for traineeships. It was found that white students were six times more likely to be offered a place (*The Independent*, 24 April, 1994: 5).

The concern at the shortage of black administrators, teachers and trainee students is also being felt in the United States. Cooper (1988: 124) voiced this anxiety in the editorial comments in the Journal of Negro Education. He wrote: 'Black children's achievement is significantly affected by teachers' perceptions, as well as by their own self-perception... In our changing and pluralistic society...it is incumbent on the society to prepare and retrain Black teachers and administrators for future service.'

Such sentiments have also been expressed in this country by various bodies (see Rampton Report, 1981; House of Commons Select Committee, 1973; Mortimer, 1989). There are some commendable initiatives being undertaken by the local education authorities and teacher training institutions. Birmingham LEA, for instance, has appointed a special project officer to increase the recruitment of ethnic minority teachers and student teachers. She has been talking to ethnic minority sixth-formers, parents and experienced black and Asian teachers and head teachers to formulate a coherent policy for the city's recruitment drive. Kingston University has an action research programme to increase the number of ethnic minority teachers (see *TASC*, February, 1994: 6). Here, the researchers have worked out a four-phase programme for the study. It includes identifying ethnic minority students and recent graduates who show interest in teaching, and finding out students' need for possible support in their studies. They also have started a mentor scheme in which ethnic students will shadow an ethnic teacher of the same group. Bradford and Ilkely Community College (see *Times Educational Supplement*, February 25, 1994: 16), with the support of the city council, has started a programme where two-year bilingual classroom assistants can gain a Certificate for Mature Students. This will entitle them to degree level matriculation. This is a good example of a special access course, the type recommended by the Commission for Racial Equality (see Ranger, 1988: 70) and the Swann Committee (DES, 1985: 605–9). The Higher Funding Council has sponsored a number of research projects which will explore ways of recruiting more teachers from the ethnic minorities (see *TASC*, Winter and Spring issues, 20 and 21).

There is another angle to the recruitment issue. Asian parents are more willing for their daughters to attend local Higher Educational Institutions and generally tend to think that the teaching profession is more for their girls than for boys. There is some evidence to suggest (Thornely & Siann, 1991; Wade & Souter, 1991; Afshar, 1989; Osler, 1989) that Asian girls, especially from Muslim and Sikh families, are doubly disadvantaged and are not realising their full educational and economic potential. They suffer in two ways: the sexist attitudes of their own community; and racism from the white society.

The primary focus of the project was to discover interviewees' perceptions, opinions and perspectives. To this end, I think, the project had a high degree of success. Whether the knowledge derived from therein will have any impact in improving the predicament of Asian and other ethnic minority teachers is hard to say. But of one thing I am convinced: in social sciences and in Education the matters under debate are very complex, and the sad truth is that interested groups are often prone to simplify matters (to seek linear causality) to their own advantage, thus reducing the possibilities of consensus and thereby concerted action. Witness the current debate on the possible links between violent and aggressive behaviour by children and young people on the one hand and their exposure to violence on TV and 'video-nasties' on the other. Likewise on the issue of lack of promotion of Asian teachers, there has been a polarisation of opinion from blaming racism to blaming Asian teachers for their inadequacies in English, their poor academic qualifications and traditional attitudes.

At the time of writing the apartheid regime in South Africa is about to give way to a democratically elected government, thus restoring hope and optimism in ultimate human justice and fair play. It is the fervent hope of the writer that due cognisance will be taken of all the emerging factors in order to secure justice and to promote equality of opportunity for the ethnic minority teachers.

References

ANWAR, M. 1979, *The Myth of Return: Pakistanis in Britain*. London: Heineman.

ANWAR, M. and ALI, A. 1987, *Overseas Doctors: Experience and Expectations*. London: Commission for Racial Equality.

AFSHAR, H. 1989, Gender roles and the moral economy of kin among Pakistani women in West Yorkshire. *New Community* 15, 211–25.

BAGLEY, C. 1969, A survey of problems reported by Indian and Pakistani immigrants in Britain. *Race* 11 (1), 65–76.

BAKER, C. 1985, *Aspects of Bilingualism in Wales*. Clevedon: Multilingual Matters.

BELLIN, W. 1995, (in press) Psychology and bilingual education: Intelligence tests and the influence of pedagogy. In B. JONES, B. and P.A.S. GHUMAN (eds) *Education, Bilingualism and Identity*. Cardiff: The University of Wales Press.

BENNET, N. 1976, *Teaching Styles and Pupil's Progress*. London: Open Books.

BERLIN, I. 1990, *The Crooked Timber of Humanity*. London: John Murray.

BLAIR, M. 1992, Black teachers and teacher education. *Education Review* 6 (2), 24–7.

BOURNE, J. 1989, *Moving into the Mainstream. LEA Provision for Bilingual Pupils*. Windsor: NFER-Nelson.

BRAND, J. 1972, Development of a special course for immigrant teachers. *Educational Review* 24 (Feb.), 145–54.

BRAR, S. H. 1991, Unequal opportunities: The recruitment, selection and promotion prospects for black teachers. *Evaluation and Research in Education* 5 (1&2), 35–47.

COOPER, C. C. 1988, Implications of the absence of black teachers/administrators on black youth. *Journal of Negro Education* 57 (2), 123–4.

COMMISSION FOR RACIAL EQUALITY 1989, *Evidence Submitted to the Education, Science and Arts Committee of the House of Commons: The Supply of Teachers for the 1990s*. London: CRE.

CUMMINS, J. 1988, From multicultural to anti-racist education: An analysis of programmes and policies in Ontario. In T. SKUTNABB-KANGAS, and J. CUMMINS (eds) *Minority Education* (pp. 127–60). Clevedon: Multilingual Matters.

DEPARTMENT OF EDUCATTION AND SCIENCE (DES) 1985, *Education for All* (The Swann Report). London: HMSO.

DRURY, B. 1991, Sikh girls and the maintenance of an ethnic culture. *New Community* 17 (3), 387–400.

DUNCAN, C. 1992, The call for separate schools. In B. DRURY (ed.) *Education, The Education Reform Act (1988) and Racial Equality: A Conference Report* (Occasional Paper in Ethnic Relations No.7). Warwick: Centre for Research in Ethnic Relations, University of Warwick.

EGGLESTON, J. 1992, Can anti-racist education survive the 1988 Education Act? In B. DRURY (ed.) *Education, The Education Reform Act (1988) and Racial Equality: A*

Conference Report (Occasional Paper in Ethnic Relations No.7). Warwick: Centre for Research in Ethnic Relations, University of Warwick.

FRYER, P. 1992, *Staying Power: The History of Black People in Britain*. London: Pluto Press.

GHUMAN, P.A.S. 1975, *The Cultural Context of Thinking: A Comparative Study of Punjabi and English Boys*. Slough: National Foundations for Educational Research.

— 1978, A comparative study of British and Punjabi trainee teachers' attitudes to children's learning and thinking. *Proceedings of the IACCP Conference* (pp. 56–62).

— 1980, Bhattra Sikhs in Cardiff: Family and kinship organisation. *New Community* 8 (3), 308–16.

— 1989, Best or worst of two worlds: A study of Asian adolescents. *Educational Research* 33 (2), 121–32.

— 1991, Have they passed the cricket test? A qualitative study of Asian adolescents. *Journal of Multilingual and Multicultural Development* 12 (5), 327–46.

— 1993, *Coping With Two Cultures: A Study of British Asians and Indo-Canadian Adolescents*. Clevedon: Multilingual Matters.

GHUMAN, P.A.S. and MAKIN, H. 1994, A study of self-conceptualization of two student groups in their first year of post-compulsory education. *The Welsh Journal of Education* May, 18–25.

GIBSON, A. M. 1988, *Accommodation without Assimilation*. Ithaca and London: Cornell University Press.

GILROY, B. 1975, *Black Teacher*. London: Cassell.

HAMMERSLEY, M. and ATKINSON, P. 1983, *Ethnography: Principles in Practice*. London: Tavistock Publications.

HERO, D. 1992, *Black British, White British: A History of Race Relations in Britain*. London: Paladin.

HILSUM, S. and START, B. K. 1974, *Promotion and Careers in Teaching*. Windsor: NFER Publishing Company.

HOLMES, COLIN 1988, *John Bull's Island: Immigration and British Society 1871–1971*. London: Macmillan.

HOLMES, CAROLYN 1978, Please adjust your approach. *Times Educational Supplement* 1 September, p. 11.

HOUSE OF COMMONS SELECT COMMITTEE ON RACE RELATIONS AND IMMIGRATION, 1973, *Education*. London: HMSO.

JACKSON, M. 1975, The DES didn't seem to know much about us: A TES report on immigrant teachers. *Times Educational Supplement* 18 July, pp. 8–9.

JONES, T. 1993, *Britain's Ethnic Minorities: An Analysis of the Labour Force Survey*. London: Policy Studies Institute.

JUNG, C.G. 1988, *Four Archetypes*. London: Ark Paperbacks.

KERLINGER, N. 1970, *Foundations of Behavioural Research*. London: Holt, Rinehart and Winston.

LYONS, G. 1981, *Teacher Careers and Career Perceptions*. Windsor: NFER-Nelson.

MACLEAN, R. 1992, *Teachers' Career and Promotion Patterns: A Sociological Analysis*. London: The Falmer Press.

MOOLLA, N. 1991, It's good character building stuff. *Multicultural Teaching* 9 (3), 23–4.

MORRISON, A. and McINTYRE, D. 1969. *Teachers and Teaching*. London: Penguin Education.

MORTIMORE, P., SAMMONS, L. S., LEWIS, D. and ECOB, R. 1989, *School Matters: The Junior Years*. Wells: Open Books.

MORTIMER, T. 1989, Equal opportunities for Black teachers: The role of the NUT. *National Union of Teachers Educational Review* 3 (2), 27–31.

MUKHERJEE, K.C. 1969, The examination stranglehold in India. *The World Year Book of Education*. London: Evans Brothers.

OSLER, A. 1989, *Speaking Out: Black Girls in Britain*. London: Virago Upstarts.

PAREKH, B. 1993, The heremenuetics of the Swann Report. In D. GILL and B. MAYOR (eds) *Racism and Education: Structures and Strategies*. London: Sage in Association with the Open University.

RAKHIT, A. 1989. A career experience of Asian female teachers: A case study approach. Unpublished MEd thesis, University of Warwick.

RAMPTON REPORT, 1981, West Indian children in our schools. Interim Report of the Committee of Inquiry into the Education of Children from Ethnic Minority Groups, Session, 1980–81. London: HMSO.

RANGER, C. 1988, *Ethnic Minority School Teachers*. London: Commission for Racial Equality.

REX, J. 1985, *The Concept of a Multicultural Society* (Occasional Papers in Ethnic Relations, No. 3, ESRC). Warwick: Centre for Research in Ethnic Relations.

ROSE, E.J.B. and ASSOCIATES, 1969, *Colour and Citizenship: A Report on British Race Relations*. London: Oxford University Press.

SCHOOLS COUNCIL REPORT, 1981, *Multi-ethnic Education: The Way Forward* (Pamphlet 18). London: Schools Council.

SEARLE, P. and STIBBS, A. 1989, The under representation of ethnic minority students in post-graduate teacher training. *New Community* 15 (2), 253–60.

SIKES, J.P., MEASOR, L. and WOODS, P. 1985, *Teacher Careers: Crises and Continuities*. London: The Falmer Press.

SINGH, R. 1988, *Asian and White Perceptions of the Teaching Profession*. Bradford: Bradford and Ilkley Community College.

SINGH, R., BROWN, T. and DARR, A. 1988, *Ethnic Minority Young People and Entry to Teacher Education*. Bradford: Bradford and Ilkley Community College.

SIRAJ-BLATCHFORD, I. 1991, A study of black students' perceptions of racism in initial teacher education. *British Educational Research Journal* 17 (1), 35–50.

SPENCER, D. 1989, *Times Educational Supplement* 5 May, p. A18.

SKUTNABB-KANGAS, T. 1988, Multilingualism and the education of minority children. In T. SKUTNABB-KANGAS and J. CUMMINS (eds) *Minority Education* (pp. 9–44) Clevedon: Multilingual Matters.

SMITH, D.J. and TOMLINSON, S. 1989, *The School Effect. A Study of Multi-racial Comprehensives*. London: Policy Studies Institute.

STEINER-KHAMSI, G. 1990, Community languages and anti-racist education: The open battlefield. *Educational Studies* 16 (1), 33–47.

STONES, M. 1980, *The Education of the Black Child in Britain: The Myth of Multicultural Education*. London: Fontana.

STOPES-ROE, M. and COCHRANE, R. 1990, *Citizens of this Country: The Asian-British*. Clevedon: Multilingual Matters.

TAYLOR, J. M. with HEGARTY, S. 1985, *The Best of Both Worlds...?: A Review of Research into the Education of Pupils of South Asian Origin*. Windsor: NFER-Nelson.

TAYLOR, W. H. 1990, India's National Curriculum. *Comparative Education* 27 (3), 325–34.

THORNLEY, P.E. and SIANN, G. 1991, The career aspirations of south Asian girls in Glasgow. *Gender and Education* 3 (3), 237–48.

TIZARD, B., BLATCHFORD, P., BURKE, J., FARQUHAR, C. and PELWIS, I. 1988, *Young Children at School in Inner City*. London: Lawrence Erlbaum Associates Publishers.

TROYNA, B. 1991, Underachievers or underrated? The experiences of pupils of South Asian origin in secondary school. *British Educational Research Journal* 17 (4), 361–75.

TROYNA, B. and HATCHER, R. 1992, *Racism in Children's Lives*. London: Routledge.

TOSI, A. 1988, The jewel in the crown of the modern prince: The new approach to bilingualism in multicultural education in England. In T. SKUTNABB-KANGAS and J. CUMMINS (eds) *Minority Education* (pp. 79–102). Clevedon: Multilingual Matters.

VERMA, K. G. 1992, Cultural and religious diversity within the National Curriculum. In B. DRURY (ed.) *Education, The Education Reform Act (1988) and Racial Equality: A Conference Report* (Occasional Paper in Ethnic Relations No. 7). Coventry: Centre for Research in Ethnic Relations, University of Warwick, Coventry.

— 1994. Inter-ethnic relationships in school: The report based on a study of schools in Greater Manchester (Abstracts). Manchester: School of Education, University of Manchester.

WADE, B. and SOUTER, P. 1991, *Continuing to Think: The British Asian Girl*. Clevedon: Multilingual Matters.

WALKER, R. 1981, On the uses of fiction in educational research. In D. SMETHERHAM (ed.) *Practising Evolution*. Driffield: Nofferton.

WOODS, P. 1985, Conversations with teachers: Some aspects of life-history method. *British Educational Research Journal* 11 (1), 13–16.

WRIGHT, C. 1985, School processes: An ethnographic study. In J. EGGLESTON, D. DUNN and M. ANJELI (eds) *Education for Some*. Stoke: Trentham Books.

— 1987, Black students, white teachers. In B. TROYNA (ed.) *Racial Inequality in Education*. London: Tavistock.

— 1993, Early education: Multi-racial primary school classrooms. In D. GILL and B. MAYOR (eds) *Racism and Education: Structures and Strategies*. London: Sage in Association with the Open University.

ZEC, P. 1993, Dealing with racist incidents in schools. In A. FYFE and P. FIGUEROA (eds) *Education for Cultural Diversity: The Challenge for a New Era*. London: Routledge.